Dr. Orman's

LIFE CHANGING
ANGER CURE

Eliminate Unwanted Anger, Without Anger Management,
So You Can Be Happier, Healthier,
& Don't End Up Alone

Dr. Mort Orman, M.D.
World's Leading Anger Elimination Expert

RED AUSSIE
— PUBLISHING —

Contact the Publisher:
Red Aussie Publishing
Phoenix, Arizona
redaussiepublishing@gmail.com
www.RedAussiePublishing.com

ISBN: 978-1-990090-16-5

In Association With:
TRO Productions, LLC
706 Concha Drive
Sebastian, Florida 32958

DISCLAIMERS AND LEGAL NOTICES

The author and publishers of this book have strived to be as accurate as possible in this informational product. While all attempts have been made to verify the information herein, there is no warranty either expressly stated or implied of complete or permanent accuracy, as knowledge does evolve and change.

The author, publishers, and any subsequent distributors of this work assume no responsibility for any errors, assumptions, or interpretations made as a result of consuming this information. Readers are solely responsible for how they choose to understand and/or make use of this information.

Please use prudent judgment in attempting to apply any strategies, exercises, or other recommendations suggested herein. Any perceived slights of specific persons, peoples, or organizations are unintentional.

This book is not intended as a substitute for professional medical or psychological advice or treatment when these may be needed. If medical, psychological, or other expert advice or treatment is needed, the services of an appropriate professional should be sought.

If you suffer from very severe anger or rage problems or any other serious mental or physical health condition, the advice in this book may not be appropriate or sufficient for you. If you are not already doing so, you are hereby advised to consult and work with an experienced mental health professional or medical professional.

If you believe that your anger symptoms or problems are beginning to get worse as you read this book, stop reading it immediately and consult a trained health professional.

Dr. Mort Orman is a board-certified Internal Medicine physician. As a medical professional, he has successfully helped and coached people to overcome their anger and stress-related problems for over 40 years. However, he is not a licensed nor a practicing mental health professional. As such, each individual needs to personally assess and evaluate all suggestions and advice noted in this book.

Bottom line: you are 100% responsible for how you interpret and make use of the information in this book. So please do so wisely.

RED AUSSIE
— PUBLISHING —

FREE DOWNLOADABLE GIFTS

(For Checking Out This Book)

INSTRUCTIONS: Go to http://BestAngerCure.com to access any or all of the following free downloadable gifts:

- Free video—How this book will help you eliminate unwanted anger
- Free video—Why managing anger is not your best coping strategy
- Free digital book PDF download—The Art of True Forgiveness (by Dr. Orman and presently for sale on Amazon)
- Free 1-page downloadable PDF—"20 Huge Things Humans Have Been Wrong About"
- Free video—short tribute video Dr. Orman made for his mother and played at her funeral.

This book is dedicated to the many courageous clients I've served over the years who dared to dream of an anger-free life and took the steps to make it a reality.

Table of Contents

Important Note To Readers

Throughout this book, when I use the term "anger," I refer to all varieties of this emotion, from mild irritation and day-to-day annoyances to full-blown rage and everything in between.

Also, whenever I talk about "eliminating anger," please understand I'm talking about eliminating unwanted or damaging anger, not all anger, and certainly not any anger that may be positive, beneficial, or useful in your life.

Some people believe "all emotions should be embraced and valued." That would be a noble stance, except that much of our anger causes enormous pain, suffering, division, hostility, and other unwanted problems for ourselves and those we live with, work with, and care about deeply.

We shouldn't embrace damaging or potentially harmful anger in our lives. We shouldn't manage it either. We should get rid of unwanted anger and learn how to stop getting angry in the first place, which is what this book teaches you how to do.

Anger, Bullshit, and You

"*One of the most salient features of our culture is that there is so much bullshit.*" Harry G. Frankfurt, Professor of Philosophy Emeritus at Princeton University and author of the book *On Bullshit* (2005).

In our daily lives, there is an ever-present force—bullshit. The word "bullshit" might ruffle a few feathers, perhaps even stir discomfort.

However, I love the term and use it frequently because, in its unique way, it captures something profound that echoes throughout our world and resonates within each of us.

"Bullshit" signifies something precise and palpable. This term points directly to a significant phenomenon in both our external reality and deep within ourselves. It stands for falsehoods, deception, misinformation, fake news, distorted research, erroneous memories, baseless assumptions, flawed beliefs, misguided perceptions, and a plethora of narratives crafted to deceive.

If you find yourself perturbed, angered, or offended by my recurrent use of "bullshit" in this book, I ask your indulgence. Rest assured that by journey's end, your discomfort may shift.

You might even transform your discomfort into a profound discontent with the lies and deceit that surround us daily—some we tell ourselves, and others are served to us, knowingly or unwittingly, by external sources. This pervasive and disempowering process has become a relentless force in our lives. But we can fight back.

What does bullshit have to do with anger and how you can stop getting angry, so you can be happier, healthier, and not end up alone?

One objective of this book is for you to begin linking the concept of "BULLSHIT" with the visceral reactions and feeling states that ANGER evokes in your body. This includes all forms of anger, from mild irritation and annoyance to full-blown rage and urges for physical violence.

I want you to cultivate a new and liberating habit. As soon as you start to feel the stirrings of anger within you...immediately think, "BULLSHIT."

"ANGER = BULLSHIT"

"ANGER = BULLSHIT"

"ANGER = BULLSHIT"

Plain and simple, the best way to stop getting angry, irritated, or upset is to realize that whenever you get triggered to feel angry, there is usually some type of bullshit "driving your anger bus."

Some anger experts talk about other emotions underlying and giving rise to anger—anxiety, disappointment, basic needs going unmet, and others.

While this may sometimes be true, I have found that the real culprit is BULLSHIT.

IT'S ALWAYS BULLSHIT!!!

Bullshit…stands for falsehoods, deception, misinformation, fake news, distorted research, erroneous memories, baseless assumptions, flawed beliefs, misguided perceptions, and a plethora of narratives crafted to deceive.

Dare to be bold. Choose to go against your life-long conditioning about anger. Take out a piece of paper right now and write the equation ANGER = BULLSHIT a hundred times. Do it every day until it becomes ingrained within you. Like an assignment you may have been given for misbehaving at school, this repetitive exercise will help you in ways you can't yet imagine.

After decades of personal work and honest self-examination, in addition to working with hundreds of clients, I wholeheartedly endorse the term "bullshit." I do this because it's the most potent mindset change you can make to reduce your anger.

As mentioned, if the term offends you, I extend a preemptive apology (albeit not really.) When you reach the final page, you'll likely appreciate the life changing favor I've done for you…and the world.

Preface

I n a world where truth is increasingly rare and, at times, perilous to speak, I stand before you, unafraid and unwavering, to unveil a truth about anger that has remained shrouded in silence until now.

Anger, mostly, is a bullshit emotion. With rare exceptions, the surges of irritation, frustration, or rage that course through us, whether triggered by something big or small, come from our skewed perceptions of reality.

It's like viewing the world through distorted lenses, and this warped perspective (or set of multiple warped perspectives) ignites our anger.

But wait, it gets worse. We've come to believe our anger validates the correctness of our viewpoints. Not only is our anger usually founded on falsehoods, but we compound our error by assuming our rage makes us right. It's a vicious cycle—a never-ending loop of bullshit.

This is why the world is engulfed in a seemingly unending tide of anger. It's a cycle of bullshit squared, played out repeatedly, regardless of the triggers that ignite our fury and our firm conviction of our moral righteousness.

Why I Penned These Words

I wrote these words with a singular ambition—to change the world.

My mission is to usher in a world with less anger, reduced division, diminished polarization, minimal hostility, fewer divorces, fewer estrangements, and a marked decline in senseless violence.

But it doesn't stop there. I also want to change and uplift your life. Whether you're a busy executive, a dedicated first responder, a tireless laborer, a diligent student, a devoted parent, a loving spouse, or even a cherished pet owner (believe me, pets can test our patience too), I want you to grasp the truth about anger because the truth is liberating.

When any form of anger casts a shadow over your life, you needn't endure its destructive consequences. You have a deep reservoir of power and resilience, far greater than you realize. This book will guide you to find your inner strength—your inner anger champion—and teach you how to use it.

As a physician and fellow human being, nothing would bring me greater joy than knowing I helped you to recognize the hidden causes of your anger, empowering you to seize control over them and thereby make your anger vanish at will.

I know that when you learn to eliminate your anger swiftly and stop reacting to the usual triggers from your present or past, your risk of heart attacks, strokes, and other anger-related illnesses is reduced. The specter of divorce retreats, and the likelihood that your children will inherit a legacy of anger and separation dwindles away. Your happiness, confidence, and emotional mastery will soar.

My mission is to usher in a world with less anger, reduced division, diminished polarization, minimal hostility, fewer divorces, fewer estrangements, and a marked decline in senseless violence.

As I dedicate the rest of my years to helping you and others experience these profound personal and familial transformations, I am fulfilling my greatest destiny as a physician.

That's why these words exist, and I am elated you've chosen to go on this adventure with me. Together, we will uncover the truth about anger, unshackle our lives, and build a world where deeper understanding triumphs over rage.

Introduction

Welcome to this journey to understand and conquer every kind of anger. Anger is a set of related emotions that often feel like insurmountable life obstacles.

This book will empower you with knowledge and tools to break free from the grip of anger and lead a happier, healthier, and more harmonious life.

There are six sections in this book, each providing a profound understanding of the origin of anger and a roadmap to eliminate unwanted anger from your life. Here is an outline of what lies ahead.

Part I reveals my personal struggles with anger until my mid-thirties and the damaging consequences of not understanding its true causes.

Part II chronicles my path to an anger-free life—an achievement many believe to be impossible. The good news is you don't have to follow my exact journey. There's a simpler and more direct route to reach the same destination, which I give you in this book. However, understanding my struggles with anger and how I overcame them can help you recognize that you have the same anger-eliminating capabilities within yourself.

Part III dives deep into the core of anger, unraveling its mysteries and dispelling common misconceptions. By the end of this third section, you will possess insights about human anger that elude nearly everyone, including many anger experts.

Part IV shares inspiring stories of individuals who have triumphed over anger by following my teaching principles. This includes five visionary leaders who sought my guidance to incorporate these same anger-elimination principles into their work. This will help you see the transformative potential that is in your hands.

Part V, titled "Dare To Believe…Dare To Dream…Dare To Decide," contains four additional chapters to help you apply the insights from this book to create an anger-free life.

Part VI provides more tools to help you win your battles against anger and show you how you can help create a world with less needless anger and violence.

This book will empower you with knowledge and tools to break free from the grip of anger and lead a happier, healthier, and more harmonious life.

A Little Backstory

I grew up in Baltimore, Maryland, where I was deeply influenced by the legendary football quarterback Johnny Unitas. Johnny U., as we affectionately called him, was my childhood hero. His winning attitude has been a guiding force throughout my entire life.

That spirit propelled me forward as an Internal Medicine physician for five decades and fueled my work as an anger elimination and stress elimination expert for the last forty years.

I've written 23 books and co-authored 11 more on anger and stress elimination and other health-related topics. I have also been the official sponsor of National Stress Awareness Month in the U.S. every April since 1992.

Welcome to your new life as a person who knows how to live without unwanted anger. May the inner winner within you awaken, and may the spirit of Johnny Unitas pass on to you and inspire you in your own personal anger victory.

Part I

From "Anger Elimination," Brian L. Nowell, Ph.D., 2009, 2016

"I have learned how to successfully eliminate anger from my own life and how to help anyone else who wants to get rid of his or her anger habits.

In addition to learning how to eliminate anger, I have learned many other very useful things about how to improve human happiness through my training…as a person, developmental psychologist, author, and educator."

Chapter 1

Before The Awakening

At age 28, I started a new project in the third and final year of my medical residency. I decided to learn how to play tennis.

Growing up, I had played baseball, softball, football, basketball, and even lacrosse, a Maryland favorite. Tennis was unexplored territory for me.

I joined an indoor tennis club and began lessons with a seasoned pro. I became a proficient player after a year of diligent practice and weekly guidance.

Little did I know that this newfound skill would unleash a storm within me, a tempest of emotions that would eventually shape my present-day understanding of anger.

Tennis became both a blessing and a curse. As I faced opponents of similar skill levels, I discovered a troubling pattern. Each missed shot, every lost point I believed I could have won, ignited a furious rage within me.

I directed this anger at myself, berating, cursing, and becoming a spectacle on the court, drawing disapproving glances and comments from nearby players.

As time passed, my anger escalated to angrily thrashing my tennis racquet against any inanimate object nearby. This caused many shattered racquets and costly replacements.

It was a destructive pattern, and I drew parallels between myself and the fiery tennis star John McEnroe, whose uncontrollable outbursts captivated television audiences during his prime.

This was not the first time this pattern of anger surfaced in my life. In my early twenties, anger was a frequent companion while attending Duke University and later attending medical school at the University of Maryland in Baltimore. This felt like a stark departure from the relatively anger-free years of my youth.

Also in my twenties, my anger found other targets—my parents, my younger sister, and even my beloved dogs. I experienced bouts of anger with my friends and, most detrimentally, with all of my romantic partners.

In my relationships with women, each one initially filled with so much hope and promise, the pattern repeated, leaving a string of broken hearts, including my own, and a trail of emotional wreckage.

While I was fortunate my anger hadn't taken a toll on my physical health, and I had no children to inflict it on, it exacted a heavy toll in other parts of life. Most significantly, it chipped away at my self-image and self-respect, two pillars that had always sustained me.

I was accustomed to winning in most of life's arenas. Still, my battle with anger, despite my best efforts and strategies, was a frustrating cycle of repeated failure and suffering. I found myself at the mercy of my emotions, a feeling of powerlessness I despised.

Things got so bad during my third year of medical school that I made the decision to seek therapy. This felt like a painful surrender, an admission of personal weakness and defeat.

I did it anyway. Therapy provided some value and support. However, even after years of weekly sessions, I remained an angry and anxious individual.

As far as I could see, I would be shackled to anger for the rest of my days. I was convinced this was the bottom-line truth about me. My experiences thus far provided no glimpse or hope of any different possibility.

Things got so bad during my third year of medical school that I made the decision to seek therapy. This felt like a painful surrender, an admission of personal weakness and defeat.

Little did I know I was about to reshape this belief and fundamentally alter the direction of my life. In a short time, I would heal myself of these explosive anger outbursts.

This book will show you how I achieved this transformation forty years ago and how you, too, can take your own journey toward anger mastery.

This learning will be most effective if I first share a few more examples of how anger manifested in my life so you can see no matter how deep the problem runs, or how painfully it shows up for you, mastery is possible.

Chapter 2

Anger at My Sister

I mentioned my childhood seemed relatively anger-free. As I have learned more about this, I recognized this was not entirely true. Anger had been lurking for me, not as the monstrous force it would later become, but quietly simmering beneath the surface.

There was a deep rivalry between my sister (only sibling) and me. She was five years younger, so the initial manifestations were not remarkable. But as we grew older, our paths diverged drastically.

I followed a path of self-discovery and personal growth, embracing self-awareness and self-responsibility. My sister found solace in denial and evading accountability.

These contrasting approaches inevitably led to explosive clashes because I had not yet mastered the anger curriculum on my path. One such confrontation is vividly etched in my memory.

One Sunday afternoon, during a holiday gathering with some relatives at our small family home, my sister and one of our cousins and I sat around the dining room table, engrossed in a discussion about money and finances. Others were in pleasant conversation in the adjacent living room.

I sat on one side of the dining room table, directly across from my sister, with our cousin sitting nearby at the head. At one point, my sister made a statement that seemed utterly detached from reality, and my patience waned. I disagreed and told her so, and it escalated from there.

My sister vehemently stood her ground, doubling down on her perspective, and I could not contain my frustration. Pent-up anger surged within me and without warning, I rose from my chair, leaned forward halfway across the table, and let loose a burst of fiery emotion.

My voice rose to a thunderous crescendo as I berated my sister for her blatant irresponsibility. My shouting drowned out everything else and captured the attention of everyone in the next room. This sudden, unexpected escalation caused great alarm.

Concerned relatives rushed to the scene, fearing a catastrophe. They managed to quell the immediate storm, but the embers of my anger continued to smolder.

Pent-up anger surged within me and without warning, I rose from my chair, leaned forward halfway across the table, and let loose a burst of fiery emotion.

It was a moment of internal reckoning like nothing I had ever experienced. It served as stark evidence that my relationship with anger was far from ordinary. Even so, I brushed it off, chalking it up as an atypical event, and life resumed its usual rhythm.

Anger at My Parents

My parents had a special place in the intricate tapestry of my emotional landscape. Our love-hate relationship reached its zenith during my teenage years, and it was peppered with conflicts typical of parent-teen dynamics. There were arguments over curfews, car privileges, and other inevitable power struggles that adolescence brings.

My father, a gentle and honorable man, seemed to understand me better because of our shared passion for sports. His firm yet fair approach to parenting left a lasting mark on me.

My mother presented a different challenge. She had a loving and caring nature, but her insecurities and anxieties caused friction between us.

As I matured and asserted my independence, she couldn't keep pace with my growth. She continued to treat me like a child, offering unsolicited advice and attempting to force food upon me at every opportunity. My repeated attempts to communicate my changing needs, as well as my strong desire to have her change her behavior all failed, and anger and frustration followed.

When I left for college, I escaped these tense situations, but the summers I spent at home brought back my sense of dread. When I entered medical school, I rented my own apartment, and this distanced me from the problem further.

Still, before every family get-together, my stomach churned in anticipation of the clashes with my mother I knew were coming.

This tension with my mother finally came to a head during my second year of medical residency.

A minor head cold had me resting at my apartment when a phone call from my mother took an ugly turn. During our conversation, she sensed my nasal congestion and started offering me medical advice, seemingly oblivious to my current professional status and expertise.

Did she not know I was caring for critically ill patients in the hospital?

I couldn't believe she continued to treat me like a child, particularly in matters of my own health. It was a tipping point, and I firmly declared over the phone, "That's it. I don't want to speak with you ever again. I want you out of my life."

I hung up the phone, confident in my decision. A few minutes later, my father called, inquiring about the turmoil I had caused. I explained my stance, assuring him that my issues were with mother and not him. I wanted to maintain our relationship, but my mother was no longer welcome.

To my disappointment, my father explained that it didn't work that way. "We are a package deal, son," he said and then explained that if I chose to cut ties with my mother, I would also lose contact with him.

It was a tough pill to swallow, but I accepted it. I was finally on my own, liberated from their influence, even if it came at a price.

For the next **seven years**, despite living just a few miles away from my parents in the same city, I maintained my silence and distance.

"That's it. I don't want to speak with you ever again. I want you out of my life."

While this decision had its merits for me in terms of my personal growth, it undoubtedly caused pain and heartache for my mom and dad. However, my developmental needs at that time took precedence over their hurt feelings.

As we move deeper into eliminating anger, I will share with you how I eventually dismantled the walls of anger that separated me from my parents. But before that, there's more to tell, more background to unveil, and more of a story to explore.

Chapter 3

As my medical career unfolded, my anger found additional avenues, branching out in diverse and unpredictable ways.

I experienced a growing frustration whenever I encountered what I perceived as stupidity, foolishness, or inconsideration.

There's an abundance of such behaviors in our world, right? These actions seem devoid of common sense or empathy and thus become sparks to ignite anger.

This anger wasn't confined to my personal life. It also showed up in my professional world, tarnishing my interactions with some of my patients. There were moments when I found myself seething with irritation when individuals chose to disregard my medical advice or make decisions that were detrimental to their well-being.

For example, I would routinely urge patients to exercise to improve their health, only to be met with strong resistance. When I saw them again, still stagnant in their ways, a spark of anger ignited within me.

I justified this emotional reaction with the belief that my anger could serve as a catalyst for them to change. Still, more often than not, it proved insufficient to motivate them.

> **In those early years of my medical practice, I believed I had a firm grasp on the sources of my anger—stupid people doing stupid things.**

My temper also flared when people made imprudent choices, particularly when it involved matters of life and death. Some would adamantly refuse essential medical tests—CT scans, MRIs, even heart catheterizations. I understood their right to refuse these procedures, but it still incensed me.

In those early years of my medical practice, I believed I had a firm grasp on the sources of my anger—stupid people doing stupid things.

However, since then, I've come to realize my anger was never truly a product of others' actions, no matter how perplexing or foolish those actions might have appeared to me.

Instead, my anger was a product of **internal factors**: emotion-generating thoughts and behavior patterns within me (you'll learn about these later).

At that time, I was ill-equipped to identify and understand these internal causes that wreaked havoc on my emotional landscape.

This book will give you the knowledge you'll need to avoid the clueless and hapless phase I went through. By the time you reach the end of this guide, you will emerge with a clearer understanding of your own internal makeup and be equipped to navigate and master the stormy seas of anger.

Chapter 4

Have you ever known someone whose anger made inanimate objects suddenly take flight?

I've crossed paths with very few, but I had one fiery romantic relationship that taught me a special lesson about the power of anger. It was a lesson in learning to duck…and much more.

By the time I was 35, my track record with relationships, especially those with women, was a string of unhappy endings. While I can gratefully say there was no physical violence or abuse involved, there was always a plethora of arguments and bickering.

It is safe to say anger contributed to my failed relationships, not just with women but also with others I held dear.

I soon realized anger is incredibly destructive for most relationships. For many, especially married couples, anger can lead to the painful road of divorce. And when children are involved, the repercussions also ripple into their lives.

Before learning to eliminate anger and finding a lasting, harmonious relationship with my wife, Christina, in 1984, anger interfered with all my prior romantic relationships.

A few examples will illustrate the problems I experienced and provide more insight as I share my awakening.

One relationship I had during my internship and residency started well enough. She was a nursing student, and we were together for about a year. When I decided to end that relationship because we weren't really getting along, her initial calm demeanor gave way to industrial-strength anger.

Sometime later, a close high-school friend, now a dental student at the University of Maryland, introduced me to a social work student he had treated. We instantly connected, and she moved in after her lease renewal came due. While our relationship had its highs, frequent arguments and unresolved anger became a recurring theme.

Despite these frequent conflicts, my girlfriend was eager to marry, but I knew I wasn't ready. My struggles with controlling my anger were still a hurdle I couldn't clear.

Still, we lived together for two years. Ending that relationship wasn't easy, but at least it was peaceful.

The next example was with a woman I will call "the thrower." Once again, my dentist-in-training friend played matchmaker and introduced me to a woman who had just exited a relationship. After only a few weeks, we became romantically involved. When her apartment lease was up, she, too, decided to move in.

As our relationship deepened, the honeymoon phase faded, giving way to fights and arguments over trivial matters. Her temper surpassed anything I had ever encountered before, and I was ill-equipped to handle her volatile bouts of anger.

When I dared to point out her own responsibility in our disagreements, her rage would flare, and she would start hurling objects in my direction.

Thankfully, her aim could have been better, and I was never struck by any of the projectiles. Still, the threat was always present.

Looking back, I realized this tumultuous relationship taught me some crucial lessons about anger:

• Anger knows no gender boundaries; women can become just as furious as men, and sometimes even more so.

• I became skilled at the art of evasion, learning to quickly duck with remarkable agility.

• Even if it is undeniably accurate, telling the truth to someone in the throes of anger often fuels their rage.

In the chapters ahead, we'll dive into other lessons I learned from my own experiences, seeing others behavior, and the wisdom of experts in the field. For now, let's continue exploring the complexities of the emotion of anger and how to navigate its turbulent waters.

I soon realized anger is incredibly destructive for most relationships. For many, especially married couples, anger can lead to the painful road of divorce. And when children are involved, the repercussions also ripple into their lives.

Chapter 5

In my relationship with the "thrower," I uncovered another hidden truth about anger—an underlying mythology that permeates our society. It's a myth I once bought into, and you probably have, too.

This pervasive belief suggests there are only two ways to deal with anger: either we suppress it, holding it within, or we express it, releasing it out into the world.

This concept aligns with our intuitive understanding of pressure in physics.

Like heating gas in a chamber, we think there can only be two outcomes: the pressure builds up and creates turmoil if left unchecked, or it's released, alleviating the tension.

We've been cautioned that suppressing anger might harm our internal well-being, and if we store up this emotional pressure, it will inevitably "come out" at an inopportune moment.

Conversely, we've also been advised that expressing anger is a mark of emotional health and regulation. It's as if venting our frustrations externally is the ultimate solution. The world around us endorses this binary approach to anger management.

But as we move through life, we discover reality often doesn't align with this simplistic dichotomy. Yes, suppressing anger can have negative consequences, but our society also teaches us there are circumstances where it's wise to keep our emotions in check.

For instance, when angry with your boss, it might be prudent to bide your time and let the anger dissipate. The same goes for dealing with coworkers, subordinates, or customers.

In the intricate dance of marriage, expressing every minor annoyance can be counterproductive. Therefore, we develop the art of concealing feelings until they naturally subside.

Moreover, we're well aware expressing anger isn't without pitfalls. When my girlfriend hurled objects in anger, she unwittingly endorsed the notion that expressing anger is always beneficial. This philosophy did little to improve our relationship.

It's a belief so ingrained in our culture that an entire industry has emerged to teach us how to express or reduce our anger effectively. From taking deep breaths to removing ourselves from the situation, hitting pillows, punching bags, or using "I" statements instead of accusatory "you" statements, these techniques are valuable but still rooted in the same limited anger management mentality.

When my girlfriend hurled objects in anger, she unwittingly endorsed the notion that expressing anger is always beneficial...It's a belief so ingrained in our culture that an entire industry has emerged to teach us how to express or reduce our anger effectively.

What if I told you there's a third and better option that transcends the suppress-it-versus-express-it debate?

This is where I challenge the mythology (bullshit) surrounding anger management. What if you could learn to prevent anger from arising in the first place or quickly quell it whenever it starts to bubble up?

If you possessed this skill, the dilemma of suppressing or expressing anger would disappear. You could halt the anger build-up within your body, eliminating the need for management altogether.

Traditional wisdom completely overlooks this third path.

In addition, some anger experts have pointed out that expressing anger has another unrecognized drawback. Aside from the complications that arise when we express our anger poorly, which is all too common, every time we express our anger artfully, we're still essentially practicing how to be angry—not how to prevent anger in the first place, which is the core focus of this book.

Forty-plus years ago, I decided to conquer my own anger issues, not by becoming better at expressing or managing it, but **by unraveling its internal causes**.

This book shares what I learned and will teach you how to do the same. As you acquire this crucial skill set, you'll be way ahead of the curve. You will see possibilities where others see problems and live in an emotional space of peace that those around you will notice and perhaps envy.

You'll master the third and often overlooked anger-coping option, which I call "anger elimination." It's a concept most are unaware of, and many believe is impossible to achieve.

I achieved it over four decades ago and have never looked back. I've also helped countless others overcome their anger issues, and you can do the same. Together, we'll journey towards a place free from the shackles of anger, where emotional freedom awaits.

Chapter 6

Before diving into Part II, where I reveal the strategies that helped me conquer my anger issues, let's explore a few more aspects of anger.

In Chapter 7, we'll look into anger's hefty price tag, especially before we learn how to tame it.

To be fair, in this chapter, we'll explore the flip side of this emotion. There are a few positive aspects of anger we still need to discuss.

The Upside of Anger

We all know, deep down, that anger isn't just a destructive force. It has positive benefits, even though they are usually overshadowed by the more destructive side of this emotion.

Here is a partial list of some of the potential positives anger can bring:

1. **Anger as a Communication Tool**: Anger can communicate our inner feelings, letting others know when we're upset or irritated. While it's best not to rely solely on anger for this, it does serve as an alarm bell.

2. **Anger for Self-Motivation**: At times, anger can be the catalyst that propels us to make positive changes. It pushes us to seek new approaches, ask for help, or break through personal limitations. It can also motivate us to take action when we've been wronged.

3.   **Anger to Motivate Others**: Anger can influence others' behavior. Parents may use it to discipline their children, bosses to motivate employees, coaches to inspire players, or individuals to deter potential threats.

4.   **Anger to Get What We Want**: In some situations, anger can be employed strategically to manipulate or influence others. It can lead to refunds or favorable outcomes in disputes. Even just the threat of anger can be a powerful motivator.

5.   **Anger for Setting Boundaries**: Anger helps establish and maintain personal boundaries, making clear what is acceptable and what is not.

6.   **Anger for Social Change**: On a broader scale, collective anger fuels social and political movements. Throughout history, anger has driven protests and movements for justice and equality.

7.   **Anger Makes Some Feel Alive**: While many view anger negatively, some embrace it, believing it makes them feel more alive. However, this can be costly from multiple standpoints, and there are healthier ways to find vitality without relying on anger.

8.   **Anger Makes Some Feel Strong and Powerful**: Anger can be a tool for those drawn to power and dominance. Throughout history, some leaders and authority figures have used anger to assert control and dominate.

9.   **Anger as a Sign of Caring and Connection**: Some argue anger is a natural part of human relationships because we often get angry with those we care about most. This proposition is flawed because

healthy relationships don't require anger but thrive more with effective communication.

10. **Temper Tantrums**: Children learn young that anger can sway their parents. While temper tantrums usually subside as we mature, sometimes the lessons carry over into adulthood.

We all know, deep down, that anger isn't just a destructive force. It has positive benefits, even though they are usually overshadowed by the more destructive side of this emotion.

Anger and Aggression | Anger and Assertiveness

It's crucial to distinguish between anger and aggression and between anger and assertiveness. Although anger can sometimes lead to aggression or assertiveness, it is not always necessary or even required.

Consider this example from my own life: as a young little-league baseball player, I was a good fielder but a terrible hitter. I was fearful and timid at the plate, and my swings were weak and unaggressive.

However, once I became a teenager and transitioned to softball, the slower pitch speeds and my increased physical strength allowed me to become a more aggressive hitter without being driven by anger.

I wasn't angry at the ball or the pitcher; I simply enjoyed being more aggressive and, therefore, more successful.

Eventually, I became more confident and was even regarded by my peers as a "dangerous" hitter. I was now aggressively "attacking" the ball rather than cowering in fear as I had previously done.

In this example, I became highly aggressive in the context of a sport without using anger as a driving or motivating force.

In this chapter, I've shown that anger possesses some positive qualities. Recognizing these benefits can help us avoid seeing anger as an entirely destructive or negative force.

However, it's essential to remember that anger is often harmful and costly in our lives.

Chapter 7

The High Cost Of Anger

I recently met a woman at a small workshop. She shared some of her life experiences with me, including one tragic story that is appropriate here.

She is the mother of four boys. Several years ago, her oldest son was in high school and struggling with unhappiness and other emotional problems. One afternoon, she and her son got into a heated argument in the living room of their home. The son ended the argument, turned to his mother and angrily said, "I hate you." As he turned his back and walked away, his mother angrily replied, "I hate you too." The boy marched upstairs to his bedroom, found his father's gun, and shot himself dead.

If you don't think anger can be costly…think again.

As we arrive at this final chapter of Part I, we stand at the threshold of a significant transformation. In Part II, I'll unveil the precise steps I took to break free from anger's relentless grip.

You've heard my stories: the strained relationships with family, the failed romances, the frustration with myself, and the belief that anger was an unshakable part of who I was. Those were dark times, but they fueled my determination to find a way out.

Thankfully, I did find a way out, and that's why I'm writing this book—to guide you toward freedom from anger's grasp, no matter how long anger has held you hostage.

In the forty-plus years since my initial anger breakthrough, my life has been mostly anger-free and full of joy.

Now, as one last warning, I want to focus again on the high cost of unchecked anger.

The Cost Of Zero

Several years ago, I penned a paper titled "The High Cost Of Zero," not about the number zero but about the tremendous price paid by those who put zero effort, zero intention, or zero commitment into banishing anger and stress from their lives.

Many follow this path and pay a steep price for failing to take decisive action. Here are some of the costs in seven life areas, if you choose to continue living with unresolved anger.

NOTE: As you read through the list of actual and potential costs below, notice which ones concern you the most.

Mental Costs:

- Decreased focus
- Poor decision-making (especially when angry)
- Increased mistakes
- Negative thinking
- Scattered thoughts
- Lack of clarity

- Self-criticism
- Blaming self and others
- Poor leadership and role modeling
- Risk of mental illness or breakdown

Emotional Costs:

- Guilt or shame
- Depression
- Frequent anger outbursts
- Poor emotional control
- Absence of inner peace
- Rejection and alienation
- Loneliness
- Lack of joy and happiness
- Feeling worthless

Physical Costs:

- Headaches
- Tense muscles
- High blood pressure
- Indigestion
- Weight gain
- Sleep disturbances

- Inability to relax

- Fatigue and exhaustion

- Burnout

- Increased risk of heart attack or stroke

- Weakened immune system

- Vulnerability to other illnesses

- Addictions and substance abuse

- Poor self-care

Financial Costs:

- Poor business and financial decisions

- High employee turnover

- Disengaged employees

- Strained relationships with suppliers, customers, staff, and partners

- Expensive mistakes

- Increased healthcare and insurance costs

- Accidents

- Spending on calming mechanisms such as alcohol, cigarettes, medications, or drugs

Family Costs:

- Marital discord

- Strained relationships with children

- Strained relationships with in-laws
- Strained relationships with aging parents
- Elevated risk of divorce
- Loss of respect from loved ones
- Hurtful words spoken in anger
- Neglecting family needs
- Reduced intimacy and sex life
- Feeling guilty or ashamed of behavior toward family
- Loss of affection from loved ones

Social Costs:

- Reduced socializing
- Alienating friends and acquaintances
- Negatively impacting others' well-being
- Loss of respect from peers
- Others making fun of or thinking poorly of you
- Causing stress and anxiety for others
- Undermining others' self-worth

Spiritual Costs:

- Lowered self-esteem and self-love
- Pessimism
- Self-doubt

- Not adhering to core values

- Living a life without meaning or purpose

- Not supporting causes you care about

- Living a life you're not proud of

- Failing as a leader, motivator, and role model

Take a few moments to be totally honest about these anger costs, for your own benefit.

Review this list and identify any anger costs you may have experienced or could experience in the future.

If you don't think anger can be costly...

think again.

Confronting these realities isn't easy, but it's crucial. For best results, don't just think about them; write them down clearly and completely.

Telling the truth is the first and most essential ingredient to being able to eliminate all your unwanted or potentially harmful anger.

The more honest you can be about what anger has already cost you or might cost you in the future, the more open you'll be to the profound insights awaiting you in subsequent chapters.

This exercise is an excellent warm-up for Part III, "The Real Truth About Anger and What You Can Do About It." There, we'll uncover the mountains of bullshit underlying our anger and also underlying what people have been taught to believe about it.

I often refer to anger as "the bullshit emotion" because, in truth, much of our anger arises from falsehoods. The key to liberation from anger's grip, therefore…is honesty.

Remember this life changing equation: **ANGER = BULLSHIT**.

I know I haven't demonstrated this to you yet, but I will, so be patient and continue with me on this life changing journey as we move on to Part II.

Part II

Anger…Gone In A Flash

Every human has experienced feeling angry and then having their anger vanish entirely in a flash.

For example, you arranged to meet someone and told them it was essential to be on time. You show up promptly, but the other person isn't there. Ten minutes elapse, and you begin to get angry. You start imagining all sorts of ways they behaved irresponsibly. A few moments later, they arrive and have an excellent explanation for why they were delayed. As soon as you find out what really happened, your anger disappears.

In retrospect, the reason you got angry turned out to be bullshit. You didn't know it at the time, but once you know the truth, it's almost impossible to remain angry.

This simple and yet fundamental change in your view of the situation is the essence of anger elimination.

We all know it is possible for emotions to suddenly change; it is a real thing…we just never learn to make it happen on demand, which we all can do whenever we want.

Chapter 8

The Power Within

In Part II, we take a journey, starting with what I learned, and then transcending my experiences to touch the heart of what it means to grapple with anger and eventually win.

This chapter, "Unleash Your Inner Power: A Journey From Anger To Freedom," begins our voyage. It's about my evolution from a perpetually angry young doctor to a life primarily devoid of anger and filled with calmness, contentment, and joy.

It's a story about hope, resilience, and the incredible power within each of us.

You might wonder why my journey matters. After all, my story is just one among billions, and you may be thinking, "Well, that's great for you, but what does it have to do with me?" The answer is simple: it has everything to do with you.

What I discovered forty years ago shattered my firm belief that anger was a permanent part of my personality. It wasn't.

I possessed the inner power to change all along. I just didn't know I had this inner power. I also didn't know how to access it.

After years of coaching people from diverse backgrounds, I've consistently found that this same internal power to eliminate unwanted anger isn't exclusive to me—it resides in everyone.

It's a story about hope, resilience, and the incredible power within each of us.

This same inner power dwells within you whether you realize it or not.

In the words of personal development guru Tony Robbins, my role as an anger elimination coach is to help you "unleash your power within."

My journey from anger's clutches to victory over anger isn't just a tale of personal success; it's a blueprint for your triumph as well.

As we walk the path together, please pay close attention.

Not because you must navigate the exact steps I did or do things in the same sequence I did them. But because you will undergo a similar awakening process to connect with your inner superpower and learn how to apply it to eliminate unwanted and potentially harmful anger in your life.

Fortunately, after years of work, I've created a simpler, faster path that only requires a few hours, not years.

By following this shortened path to unlocking your anger elimination superpower, you will discover, as I did, that you possess not just one but many other remarkable abilities you currently don't believe you have.

Those other amazing superpowers will be topics for future books and training programs.

After years of coaching people from diverse backgrounds, I've consistently found that this same internal power to eliminate unwanted anger isn't exclusive to me—it resides in everyone.

For now, immerse yourself in my story of how I overcame anger as if it were an entertaining movie or a gripping novel, chronicling a hero eventually triumphing over an all-too-common powerful villain.

I started with a goal—to become anger-free—but achieved little to no success for many years, the obstacles seeming insurmountable.

Then, an unexpected turn of events changed everything, and I learned life lessons that destroyed my old beliefs—"I can't do it," "I don't have the power," and "I'm always going to be this way."

Liberated from these false and self-limiting convictions, I charted a new course that finally enabled me to access my dormant inner power and live a life nearly free of anger.

Everything I learned during this self-examination, you can learn about yourself and any problematic anger you might have.

Once you grasp these insights, you'll realize you and I aren't all that different.

You have the same "equipment" I had when I started on my self-improvement journey forty years ago: a human brain and a human body. Our brains and bodies have been constantly conditioned throughout our lives.

We can become aware of how our brains and bodies have been conditioned and learn how to use our inner powers to better respond to that conditioning.

What you'll witness in my story is how I cured myself of long-standing anger problems.

As you read this book and listen in your heart, you'll see how you, too, can get the same life changing rewards, because you, too, have the same internal capabilities.

Chapter 9

The story of how I transitioned from a young, angry man to a life almost free of anger begins at the beginning.

You already know the destination—a life liberated from anger's grip. But the seeds of this profound personal change were sown in my heart many years earlier, and it all began with a boyhood hero.

In recounting my story of change, there are many possible beginning points. I could start with my birth in 1948 in Baltimore, Maryland, to loving and caring parents. At that time, being born in post-WWII America was a blessing.

Or I could start with my idyllic early childhood, growing up in a stable, nurturing environment where values like education and honesty were held in high regard.

However, the key moment that set me on a path to become a physician and eventually accomplish other remarkable feats, including conquering my anger, occurred when I was just ten.

My life as a young boy was profoundly shaped by my first childhood hero. Growing up in Baltimore during the 1950s, my father and I were die-hard Baltimore Colts football fans.

My dad held two season tickets, and we attended every Colts home game together, a tradition that began in 1957, when I was nine, and continued until the team left Baltimore for Indianapolis in 1984.

During those 27 years, I missed only one home game due to a bout of chickenpox and a fever of 102 degrees. I pleaded with my parents to let me attend that game anyway, but they stood firm.

Disheartened, I listened to the game on the radio at home. (I must admit, I was very angry with my parents for restricting me that day.)

In my youthful passion for football, one player stood out above all others—Johnny Unitas, the star quarterback of the Baltimore Colts.

Johnny Unitas (1933-2002) was a Hall of Fame quarterback and one of the fiercest competitors in the sport's history. His specialty was orchestrating incredible comebacks, snatching victory from the jaws of defeat.

From that very young age, I aspired to be like Johnny U. I didn't expect to become an NFL quarterback, but I dreamed of becoming a winner in life, just like him.

As a kid, I spent countless afternoons throwing a football around with a friend after school. We'd take turns pretending to be Johnny U., with the other playing the role of Raymond Berry, his favorite receiver (also a Hall of Famer).

Johnny Unitas imparted to me and burned into my youthful heart the desire to be a winner and the blueprint for adopting a winner's mindset.

Every Sunday, he demonstrated the power of never giving up, of refusing to give in to despair regardless of the score or the odds stacked against him.

As one of his many idolizing fans, I believed that Johnny U. would find a way to win, which he did more often than not.

Watching him perform on the field and engulfing myself in his winning spirit left an indelible mark on my young, impressionable heart.

What a gift!

I'm sure he influenced countless other young minds and hearts in Baltimore and nationwide.

That experience instilled in me an unwavering commitment never to give up, even when faced with challenges and obstacles. As the years passed, I held on to that optimism, nurtured by his spirit and example.

Johnny Unitas taught me this: stay in the game and search for ways to win, even when others lose faith. Keep searching, and victory will eventually be yours.

I carried that winning spirit with me throughout my life.

As a struggling student in junior high school and in my first year of high school, I eventually invoked Johnny's spirit to become an A-student and graduate with the third-best GPA in my high school class of over 900 seniors.

I channeled that same winning spirit to excel academically in college and to emerge victorious in most sports I pursued.

I clung to my Johnny U. legacy during the formidable challenges of medical school and my grueling three years of internship and residency training. It also enabled me to become an outstanding internal medicine physician, once I opened my own private practice in Baltimore.

So, what does Johnny Unitas and his winning spirit have to do with my eventual conquest of anger?

When I first realized that anger was a major obstacle in my life—one that threatened my ability to build lasting relationships, have a family, and maintain my health—I knew I had to take action.

I set out on a mission to learn about anger and how to defeat it. I explored various anger management and stress management techniques.

Though I was diligent, these efforts offered little relief. I would wake up every day, and the same anger was still within me. It was a relentless cycle that felt like Groundhog Day, which amusingly happens to be my birthday (February 2nd).

I even sought therapy during medical school, yet the anger persisted. It was a disheartening and demoralizing experience. Despite my earnest efforts, I had never encountered such consistent failure in my life.

After years of fruitless attempts, I was on the verge of giving up. I almost surrendered to the belief that anger was an indelible part of my personality and that I was destined to be this way forever. But the spirit of Johnny Unitas, which had been with me since I was ten, refused to let me quit.

...the key moment that set me on a path to become a physician and eventually accomplish other remarkable feats, including conquering my anger, occurred when I was just ten.

I continued to search for answers, hoping for a lasting cure. Just as Johnny U. knew on the football field, I knew that victory was possible; I simply hadn't found the right path yet. The victory was out there, waiting for me to discover it. I just had to stay in the game, keep playing, and keep searching.

So, the way I eventually conquered anger began with my idolization of Johnny Unitas. Unbeknownst to me, this early influence set in motion deep unconscious forces that have guided my life to this day.

To some, it may seem like divine intervention, but for me, it was simple math:

19 into 10 = Winning

Number 19: was Johnny Unitas' football jersey number and represented his winning attitude;

Into 10: my age when I first became energized by his football prowess and his indomitable spirit;

Equals winning—a formula that shaped my life in ways I could never have imagined.

A Funny Thing Happened

At age 10, I made a secret pledge to myself to grow up to be like my hero, Johnny Unitas. If you recall, I was pretty sure I would never become a professional quarterback.

As I grew older, that pledge faded into the recesses of my mind. I rarely thought about it and never planned for it to come true. Yet, an unseen force deep inside of me must have continued to influence my life choices, even if I wasn't consciously aware of it until much later.

In my forties, sitting alone in my medical office one day during a quiet moment of self-reflection, an unexpected insight struck me like a thunderbolt.

"Holy crap," I thought to myself, "I actually did become a professional quarterback!"

I'm leading a team (my patients) against a group of formidable opponents (illness, disability, and death) poised across the "line of scrimmage" from us.

I'm calling the plays (collaboratively with my patients) and trying to lead them to victory.

Isn't life amazing how it unfolds?

Isn't it also amazing that you are here now, reading this book, soon to have your own life positively impacted by me, and indirectly by Johnny Unitas, in ways you can't yet imagine.

Chapter 10

Y ou've just heard the beginning of my journey (at age 10) to become an expert in anger elimination. Let's move ahead in the story, starting about forty years ago, to another turning point which was also aided by my boyhood hero, Johnny Unitas.

Shortly after I started my Internal Medicine practice in Baltimore in 1977, I made an important decision. I chose to invest in personal development, a choice most busy professionals then and now often neglect.

Why did I make this choice? Because I believed it would make me a better and happier person and a more effective physician.

Even though, on the surface, I appeared to be a happy and confident doctor, deep down, I struggled with many internal issues. Anxiety, an overwhelming fear of public speaking, anger that seemed beyond my control, and a heart that had been broken more times than I cared to admit.

Despite my academic, professional, financial, and sports achievements, I couldn't shake the frustration that I couldn't control my emotions.

What's more, as a physician, I noticed an obvious pattern in my patients. I could easily discern the ones dominated by anger and those naturally more even-keeled and forgiving.

Over time, I saw the consequences of anger unfold before my eyes.

In general, the anger-prone individuals suffered more heart attacks, strokes, high blood pressure, divorces, business failures, strained relationships with their children, legal troubles, and the list went on.

I was witnessing a train wreck (I could clearly see the train now) of an angry life, and I couldn't ignore that the same train was headed straight for me!

Despite the indomitable spirit of Johnny Unitas still burning within me, I might have given up hope about ever getting free of my anger had I not been confronted daily (by my patients) with the grim possibilities awaiting me if I didn't address my anger issues.

This driving force, along with Johnny U.'s never give up attitude, pushed me into the realm of personal development. I realized I had gaps in my understanding of human emotions, relationships, and the path to a happier, stress-free life that my medical training never covered.

I sensed a treasure trove of knowledge out there, waiting to be explored. I decided to invest in my own education. It was one of the best decisions I ever made, and the benefits keep coming.

Despite my academic, professional, financial, and sports achievements, I couldn't shake the frustration that I couldn't control my emotions.

Admitting I had much to learn about human emotions and human nature and having the wisdom to pursue that knowledge were two more critical steps in my journey toward an anger-free life.

In medical school, I learned about the intricacies of the human body—hearts, lungs, livers, kidneys, bones, muscles, etc. What they didn't teach us was how to understand the people who inhabited those bodies, who had dreams, emotions, opinions, egos, families, and responsibilities, and who experienced painful failures.

I sensed that to honestly care for my patients and understand my own personal challenges and my own potentials, I needed to seek this new level of knowledge.

How does this relate to you and your journey to conquer anger once and for all?

Just as I had to embrace the fact there was much about human emotions, including my personal struggle with anger, that I didn't understand, you too must acknowledge the gaps in your own understandings.

In Part III, I will provide you with crucial information about anger that was missing from your education. This information will be central in your drive to live an anger-free life.

Chapter 11

Come with me now into the unconventional, the uncharted, and the profoundly unexpected.

What I share in this chapter might seem out of place or peculiar because I'll be talking about running in a book about anger.

But I promise you, it's the pivotal story that gets to the heart of the matter—the golden key to conquering your own anger issues.

You might be thinking, "Why talk about running? I'm not interested in that at all." I wasn't either. Running was never my cup of tea. In fact, it was something I intensely despised.

But what if I told you running was my key to becoming an anger elimination expert?

What if I told you it was the catalyst for shedding the cloak of anger draped over me for so long?

Let me be crystal clear: this isn't a story about the joys of running, although it might seem that way. It's about what I discovered **within myself** through running, how it rewired my perceptions, and how it ultimately led me to conquer anger.

My Hate-Hate Relationship with Running

As I've already mentioned, in my younger days, I was a sports enthusiast. I enjoyed running, but only as part of a game. The moment it turned into exercise or a solitary activity, I detested it.

Running felt boring, painful, and akin to torture.

Marathon runners? They seemed utterly mad to me. Why endure 26 times the pain of running a mile?

When I entered medical school, I became sedentary for the first time in my life, and the pounds piled on.

Every few months, I'd muster the resolve to start a running regimen, only to quit within three days, reaffirming my belief that "running was not for me" and "I was not a runner."

After completing my medical training and dabbling in personal development work, however, something new began to brew within me.

Then It Became Real

Everything changed one evening in a crowded hotel ballroom during a relationships seminar. The speaker wasn't discussing anything even remotely related to running or exercise. Yet at one point in the evening, a voice in my head firmly declared, for no apparent reason, "You can't run a marathon."

It was a moment of uncomfortable uncertainty mixed with perplexing curiosity.

I thought, "Why is this voice telling me something I already know? Why is it trying to convince me I can't do something I already know I can't do and would never want to do anyway?"

Having worked on personal development for over a year, I wondered: Could this voice be onto something?

Could there be a hidden runner within me I don't know about?

I dismissed the notion as entirely absurd. But for the rest of the seminar, it persisted, growing stronger each time I wondered about why that voice decided to speak to me.

When I got home, I couldn't shake the question: "Could there be a natural runner inside me that I don't consciously know about?"

That night, I made an audacious decision that changed my life forever.

Despite my strong aversion to running, I resolved to sign up for running a future marathon.

The very next day, I signed up to run in the Baltimore Marathon in December 1979, just five months away.

It was a daring move that was totally unthinkable for me before that prior evening. But I wanted to put these "new age" personal development principles to the test.

Let me emphasize this: I had zero confidence in the existence of a natural runner within me. I believed running would forever be an unpleasant, painful experience. Just as I was sure I would always be an angry person. Yes, I wanted to put my new personal development insights to the test, but I was pretty sure the test would fail.

Yet, I was willing to challenge my convictions and pursue a course to discover what was true.

> ...this isn't...about the joys of running. It's about what I discovered <u>within myself</u> through running...and how it ultimately led me to conquer anger.

Wrong...Wrong...And Wrong Again

To my astonishment, I eventually found out I was wrong about everything I thought I knew about running. I created a marathon training program that worked surprisingly well, even though I was convinced it would be impossible for me to succeed.

Five months later, I completed the Baltimore Marathon comfortably in 3:48, celebrating that same evening at a dance party with friends and family that went on until midnight.

When I crossed the marathon finish line earlier that day, I can't tell you how excited, astonished, and proud I felt.

It was so mind-blowing for me that, I kid you not, when my lead foot crossed the finish line and landed on the concrete roadway just behind it, I felt as if I had just stepped down onto the surface of the moon.

For a guy who had hated running for most of his life, who found running painful and physically unpleasant, and who firmly believed he would never complete a marathon in a million-billion years, that momentous final step marked one serious life changing accomplishment.

Despite everything I thought I knew and believed about running and about myself, I had successfully transformed my hatred for running into a passionate love affair for long-distance racing.

I was now a runner, and there was no going back.

The lie about me not having the ability to enjoy running, that I had lived with and believed in for so long, had been thoroughly obliterated. In its place, the champion runner inside me had been unmasked and unleashed.

---

when my lead foot crossed the finish line…

I felt as if I had just stepped down onto

the surface of the moon.

Over the years, I ran four more full marathons, including two Boston Marathons. I also enjoyably ran over 2,000 miles a year for 25 consecutive years.

A back condition finally forced me to stop. But I still think and feel like a runner, even though now all I can do is walk.

As it turned out, much to my surprise, a natural runner was hiding inside me all along.

I didn't know he was there until 1979 at age 31.

But he eventually came out, and when he did, he has never gone back into hiding.

What's Hiding Inside You?

This profound personal breakthrough with running initiated a series of other major changes in my life, including ending my struggle with anger (I'll explain this connection in the next chapter).

Just as I discovered the hidden runner champion within me, I also figured out how to liberate my **internal anger champion** as well.

If you're grappling with anger issues, you don't need to search for a hidden runner inside. Still, you must find your internal anger champion, even if you doubt its existence.

Forty years ago, I discovered my inner anger champion, and he's still going strong. By the time you finish this book, you will meet your own.

In Chapter 12, I'll share what I learned that allowed me to transform from someone who loathed running to a passionately dedicated runner.

I will also share how my running discoveries became the key to unlocking the mysteries of my longstanding battles with anger.

I promise you, these secrets also hold the key to your anger victory as well.

By the way, the finish line for the December 1979 Baltimore Marathon was directly across from the entrance to the old Memorial Stadium on East 33rd Street.

This was the same stadium and entrance my dad and I routinely passed through to watch Johnny Unitas and the Baltimore Colts play on Sundays when I was a young boy.

This may have been a coincidence...but I doubt it.

Chapter 12

I hope the last chapter, where I detailed my "miraculous" journey from a running hater to a running lover, caused a visceral reaction within you.

I started off as a person who loathed running and believed long-distance runners belonged in mental institutions.

I ended up as one who felt a passionate love for running, viewing it as a source of pleasure, free from pain, and providing me with a wellspring of physical, mental, and spiritual benefits.

Sometimes, I still pinch myself, unable to fathom how I brought about such a major and lasting personal change.

I even question how I summoned the audacity to entertain the notion of completing a marathon, let alone signing up for one, when my self-doubt and negative self-image (as a runner) painted a wildly different picture of my capabilities.

Nevertheless, it happened. And it taught me some incredibly important things about myself and other people.

That running journey also taught me important lessons that led me to the truth about anger and how to best deal with it.

The First Revelation

The first of these lessons was that running itself WAS NOT TO BLAME for my long-standing disdain and physical discomfort. I WAS.

I had wrongly attributed my misery to running, believing it was an inherently painful and unpleasant activity. Little did I know, it all hinged on how I approached the act of running, both consciously and unconsciously.

For example, many people perceive public speaking as intrinsically stressful. This is identical to me once believing running was inherently agonizing.

I later realized that neither of these activities is innately stressful or painful; it depends on our beliefs about them and how we engage with each activity. The same is true for anger.

The Second Revelation

The next nugget of wisdom regarding anger I discovered from transforming my relationship with running was:

- *Anger isn't as uncontrollable or inescapable as it may seem.*

It's all about understanding anger correctly and employing the right strategies to mitigate it.

The Third Revelation

The third nugget of wisdom I uncovered while discovering the joys of running was:

• Often, to cure or eliminate a nagging, persistent problem like anger, we must search within ourselves for hidden aspects of the problem or unwanted situation.

For instance, running uphill is more challenging than running on level ground. Yet, most people are unaware of internal thoughts and automatic behaviors that unconsciously "click in" to make uphill running more difficult than physics would dictate.

I was oblivious to how these and other hidden factors can make running more difficult and uncomfortable than it needs to be, until I went looking for them.

To my surprise, they were there, covertly affecting my running experience.

Similarly, anger (and other emotions) have **concealed thought patterns and behavior patterns** that trigger or escalate these feelings.

Unfortunately, many of us are unaware of these **internal causes.**

Because of this, we remain helpless in the face of our emotions, even though we have the power to rise above them.

On the other hand, when you learn to identify these internal factors, magical transformations suddenly become possible.

The Fourth Revelation

The fourth nugget of wisdom I discovered while developing my love for running was:

• When working with internal causes (whether addressing running or getting angry), you must get specific.

Specificity is essential regardless of the kind of internal work you are doing.

This applies to pain, emotional suffering, relationship woes, financial struggles, or anything else. **Pinpointing internal causal patterns precisely** is the only way to address them effectively.

During my five months of marathon training, I identified over 30 specific internal thought patterns and behavior patterns that were hindering my running progress and causing me to experience running as an unpleasant activity.

For example, I realized early on that my mother's mantra "no pain, no gain" had become an unconscious directive, compelling me to push through pain and discomfort in my runs. Once I recognized this internal directive was controlling how I ran, I could take decisive action to change it.

I let go of the masochistic idea I had to endure pain to make progress and adopted a gentler approach.

I decided to focus on just completing a distance each day, starting out jogging but allowing myself the freedom to walk whenever I started to feel uncomfortable.

This approach allowed my body to adapt gradually, free from unnecessary pain, discomfort, and next-day muscle soreness. It also kept me in the game and gave me no reason to quit.

> **That running journey…taught me important lessons that led me to the truth about anger and how to best deal with it.**

Just as I learned how to successfully address hidden causes affecting my running, I later applied the same basic principles to understanding and attacking the internal causes of my anger. This eventually enabled me to discover how to quickly eliminate anger, at will.

*I created this book to guide you in **pinpointing the specific internal causes of your anger** so you can take corrective action and watch your anger dissipate quickly.*

The Fifth Revelation

• We can be wrong about many things, even when we firmly believe we are right.

Just as I once held various misconceptions about running that I believed were absolutely true, many of us also harbor false beliefs about anger.

We've been taught many things about anger that aren't really true. And much of the advice we've received on managing anger is not helpful either.

To conquer anger, we must challenge and replace some of these deep-seated anger beliefs.

This book will guide you in reshaping your beliefs about anger and provide you with knowledge and strategies to lead a more loving and peaceful life. The ultimate outcome will come over time as you apply this newfound wisdom.

Rest assured, you are in capable hands. I've successfully navigated many other huge personal changes in my life, all permanently successful.

I'm here to help you do the same.

Together, we'll uncover the power to eliminate anger, embrace positive change, and create the anger-free life you deserve.

Chapter 13

Have you ever imagined what life would be like without anger?

I don't have to imagine because, for the past forty years, I've lived a life primarily anger-free. But let's take a moment to envision it together.

Picture a life where you rarely get angry with your spouse or children. Imagine a workplace where heated arguments and frustrations are rare for you.

What if you could swiftly defuse your anger at will, whether directed at yourself, others or even those pesky slow drivers on the road?

Wouldn't that be an excellent way to live?

Of course, you'd still retain the choice to get angry when it seems appropriate, but you would no longer be held captive by your anger, dragged around at its whim.

The power to achieve this level of control over your emotions already resides within you.

Still, there's a catch—you might not know how to access it.

We have our own peculiar language in medicine and healthcare, filled with industry-specific terms like "asymptomatic," which means "without symptoms."

For instance, we might say that someone has HIV (human immunodeficiency virus) that is asymptomatic. This means they carry the virus without experiencing any noticeable illness or symptoms.

Similarly, a person can have a heart attack (myocardial infarction) without the classic chest pain or other typical symptoms, a phenomenon sometimes referred to by medical professionals as "an asymptomatic MI "or "silent heart attack."

Here's the twist: **the power of who you are as a force in the world is entirely asymptomatic.**

You can't touch, see, smell, or definitively detect your inner strengths and potentials with your senses.

They exist within you as hidden, invisible powers that only reveal themselves when you witness the results of their emergence.

Much like my own experience with running, where I discovered a hidden runner within me after years of despising the activity, your inner strength as an anger eliminator might seem elusive.

You do indeed possess this potential, but it remains hidden inside you until you bring it to the surface.

I couldn't see or feel that natural runner within me until I successfully trained for and completed my first marathon, savoring the long months of training and the 26.2 miles of the actual race.

When I looked back, however, it was clear that winning runner was always within me, yet I had to assume its presence on faith until I saw it manifest in reality.

Similarly, you already harbor the power to confront and conquer your angry impulses and feelings.

You possess this winning potential within you, even if you can't see it or feel it right now. It's an invisible force, asymptomatic until you learn to harness and express it.

If you feel skeptical, I understand.

I grappled with anger for many years with limited success. My hidden power remained asymptomatic—and therefore unknown to me—until I brought it to the surface and witnessed its transformative effects.

I know you might not share my optimism for your anger success quite yet, and that's okay; doubt is a natural response.

---

you already harbor the power to confront and conquer your angry impulses and feelings.

By the end of this book, your perspective will shift. Right now, remember three things:

1. Who you are as a potential anger eliminator is asymptomatic, meaning you won't feel it, see it, or believe it right now.

2. Who you are as an anger eliminator right now is not who you will become by the end of this book.

3. Who you become as an anger eliminator by the end of this book is nowhere near the anger eliminator you will grow into as you test out and use these principles in your life.

As you work the process I lay out for you in this book, you will be far better equipped to access your inner anger champion.

That change will benefit you, your loved ones, your coworkers, and the world at large.

In a world plagued by anger and senseless violence, your voyage through this book, and your ability to access your inner strength as an anger eliminator, will be a tremendous gift to all.

There are more powerful insights to give you about anger, but before we move forward, there's one more piece of groundwork to lay down.

In the next chapter, you'll discover this process is about more than just anger; it's also about forgiveness.

By the end of our journey together, both anger and its cousin forgiveness (including how to truly let go of the past) will no longer be a mystery to you.

Chapter 14

I n our turbulent world, two undeniable truths prevail:

1. Anger festers far more than necessary.

2. Forgiveness is a genuinely scarce commodity.

The reasons for these two truths may seem perplexing, but they aren't all that mysterious. The mystery arises from widespread misconceptions and misunderstandings about anger and forgiveness.

One aim of this book is to dispel these widespread misconceptions.

As you probe deeper into the intricacies of anger, your beliefs about it will change, leaving you with more profound and powerful understandings.

You will also discover that your newfound clarity will extend to your understanding of forgiveness.

Why Forgiveness Often Eludes Us

If you've ever been hurt, betrayed, or deceived by someone you held dear, you understand how challenging forgiveness can be.

Conversely, forgiving yourself can seem equally elusive if you've been the cause of harm or betrayal.

You might comprehend intellectually that forgiveness is a virtuous path. You may also have attempted to "let go" and move on from the past.

However, deep within, the pain, resentment, and the desire for justice or retribution often linger, no matter how fervently you try to shove those memories into oblivion.

Forgiveness has been a subject of much discussion, literature, and sermons for millennia. There is abundant advice on how to forgive and countless tales of individuals who forgave even in the face of unimaginable injustices.

Yet, despite this wealth of wisdom, genuine forgiveness remains a formidable challenge, making this facet of life seem enigmatic and bewildering.

I declare boldly that the twin enigmas of anger and forgiveness can be unraveled.

Once you understand the internal root causes of anger and activate your ability to dispel most of it, you'll also see why forgiveness often eludes us.

As you probe deeper into the intricacies of anger, your beliefs about it will change, leaving you with more profound and powerful understandings.

Without the fresh new insights about anger you'll be introduced to in Part III, ridding yourself of anger and extending forgiveness will remain tough sledding.

But, armed with these new understandings, you'll be astounded at how adept you become at both quelling anger and forgiving yourself and others.

It's a logical connection: holding onto anger makes forgiveness an uphill battle, because forgiveness requires the complete release of previously harbored anger and resentment.

They are conjoined twins.

As you learn to cast off anger, your capacity for forgiveness will flourish.

Suppose, after completing this book, you want or need more help with a difficult forgiveness challenge. In that case, I recommend reading my companion book, *The Art Of True Forgiveness*, available for purchase on Amazon.com, but also available here as a free PDF download (see Free Downloadable Gifts Page at beginning of this book).

Congratulations! You have now finished Part II.

In Part III, you will gain a new perspective on human anger and a new framework for understanding its internal causes.

In addition, you will get a simple but powerful system for using that framework to expel anger from your life.

Merely managing anger is a feeble and unsatisfying coping mechanism.

If you aspire to master the art of dealing with anger, fasten your seatbelt, and let's continue our journey together in Part III.

Part III

From "Anger The Misunderstood Emotion," Carol Tavris, 1982

Human anger is not a biological reflex like the sneeze, nor simply a reactive display designed to ward off enemies. You may become roused to anger by memories and symbols as well as by real and present dangers, and you can maintain that anger for years. Beagles, in contrast, will know by your angry voice that you are displeased with them…but they will not bite you if you insult their intelligence or ancestors. (p33)

From "Never Get Angry Again," David J. Lieberman, Ph.D., 2017

Negative emotions like impatience, insecurity, and anger dissolve— not because we fight to control our emotions but, rather, <u>because we see the situation for what it really is</u>. (p3)

NOTE: This quotation could be viewed as the short version of Dr. Orman's Life Changing Anger Cure book.

A Prelude to Part III

As we stand on the threshold of Part III, I invite you to pause and reflect with me for a moment.

Parts I and II were journeys through the landscape of personal narratives—my own struggles with anger and the personal journey I took to overcome them. These stories were shared to connect our experiences and illuminate the common thread of humanity that binds us all.

Now, we switch to a different terrain in Part III. Here, the essence shifts from storytelling to an immersive, deep-dive exploration of the mechanics of anger creation and elimination. This is where we transition from narrative to application, from tales to tactics. This section equips you with principles, strategies, and newfound insights that will allow you to master your anger and live anger-free.

As we move on to this phase, please recalibrate your mindset. Envision this part as constructing a new conceptual foundation within you, brick by conceptual brick. Each chapter is meticulously designed to lay down one or more key elements, creating a robust understanding upon which you will continue to build.

I urge you to savor this journey and move with deliberation and mindfulness. The allure to skip ahead to the seemingly "exciting parts" might be strong, but remember, every element is crucial. Each concept and principle unfolds gradually, revealing the grand tapestry of a new understanding and change.

Also, don't be surprised if you need to read parts or entire chapters of Part III two or more times before they begin to sink in. Since I am introducing new ways of thinking about anger that might be discordant or divergent for you, your brain may need several "passes" over the content in order for it to settle down.

In the revelations to come in this crucial portion of the book, the Internal Anger Elimination Framework and the Ultimate Anger Elimination System will be unveiled. These are not mere tools but gateways to a deeper comprehension of anger's intricate dance and your capacity to eliminate it. By understanding the philosophies and principles that underpin these systems, you will be armed with more than just tactics; you will possess uncommon wisdom.

Looking ahead, Part IV will weave us back into the realm of stories—tales of real individuals whose lives have been transformed by the principles you are about to learn. Then, in Part V, we go even deeper, offering additional insights to enrich your journey.

Our two concluding chapters in Part VI aim to inspire and invigorate you, encouraging you to adopt this transformative approach to anger and become a beacon for others.

In a world thirsting for peace and understanding, the need for this profound shift has never been more urgent. Let's embrace this critical part of our journey with open hearts and minds, ready to reshape our lives and, perhaps, the world itself.

Chapter 15

Welcome to Part III, where you will transform your relationship with anger and learn how to free yourself from it. In the following chapters, you'll discover a fresh perspective on this complex emotion that has often eluded many anger experts.

In this section, you'll be introduced to a simple and powerful framework and a powerful associated system that will allow you to uncover the causes of your anger and do something about them.

With this new awareness, you'll conquer your anger, gain the ability to control it, eliminate its disruptive presence, and banish any stress it brings.

Once you grasp the true origins of your anger, I can promise that you can create a happier, healthier existence and avoid the pitfalls that lead to estrangements, especially in your closest relationships.

There are many benefits to living an anger-free life, and you can surely imagine the wonderful rewards that will come.

However, you may still need to learn a secret ingredient to anger elimination success. It all boils down to two fundamental truths.

Let me set the stage.

You already know about my turbulent history with anger in my twenties and early thirties. You know how my path led me to the world of personal development and, ultimately, to a deep connection with long-distance running.

This odyssey gave me profound insights that enabled me to live the last four decades with minimal anger and stress. I've also had the privilege of helping many others achieve the same happiness and fulfillment without sacrificing their goals, health, families, or productivity.

Many argue such a transformation is impossible, but those skeptics are unaware of the truth.

You may not personally know many individuals (yet) who have successfully transitioned from being perpetually angry to being completely free of anger and reveling in their newfound contentment. I'm one of those people, and I wrote this book to share my journey.

Reflecting on my arduous path four decades ago, I realized **two fundamental truths** made all the difference. In this chapter, I will lay those truths bare because they represent both the essence of this book and the heart of my expertise in helping others.

At the core, what you must do to conquer your anger and emerge victorious is quite simple. You may not believe it right now, and that's okay. Believing in yourself and just being open to the possibility that you may have an anger champion lying dormant within you is what truly matters.

I've emphasized that you absolutely possess the ability to transform your relationship with anger. I've also hinted at the crucial insights about anger you're likely missing. This book—especially Part III—will fill in those gaps.

When I finally left my anger issues behind, I took a retrospective look. I identified two key insights that eluded me during my years of struggle. These key insights were the missing pieces of the anger puzzle—the anger mystery—that kept me trapped.

I recognized whenever I experienced anger, big or small, one of two things—or sometimes both—were going on inside me.

So, what are these two critical revelations?

First, when I was angry, there was a high probability **I was wrong** about something.

I might have made erroneous assumptions, misinterpreted situations, unfairly judged others, or seen things through a distorted lens. It's a part of our human nature to make these mistakes, and the tricky part is this...

In the heat of anger, *we believe we're absolutely right when, in fact, we're often wrong.*

---

whenever I experienced anger... one of two things—or sometimes both—were going on inside me.

Remember how I was completely wrong about my aversion to running and how I attributed my negative views (and unpleasant experiences) to the activity of running itself? It was only later I realized I was responsible for making running an unpleasant experience in more than 30 different ways.

That's the type of "wrongness" I'm talking about—subtle and insidious, lurking in the background, inflicting pain and suffering on our lives in ways we don't usually notice.

Second, anger arises when we **adopt flawed philosophies**. Here are some examples:

• Suppose you believe life should always be fair. When it isn't and you become indignant, you're operating with a misguided philosophy.

• If you perceive yourself as either oppressed or an oppressor, either philosophy in our modern era is likely flawed.

• If you believe people should always treat you kindly because you're good-hearted, that doesn't happen. Another flawed philosophy.

Wrongness and misguided philosophies are prime catalysts for anger, and they have been since the dawn of our species.

What does it mean when I say anger stems from being "wrong" or having a "bad philosophy"?

In the first place, this book will show you that most of our anger gets generated from internal wrongness and/or bad philosophies (more to come on this soon).

Unfortunately, when we are caught up in the emotion of anger, we're oblivious to our errors and firmly believe our perceptions, thoughts, and feelings are justified.

This is actually another common form of "wrongness" that festers in the background, causing additional pain, suffering, and persistent anger.

As you keep reading, I hope you have a revelation similar to mine, where you realize much of your anger is internally caused by what I affectionately call "bullshit"—a combination of wrongness and misguided philosophies.

When you begin to see this is the crux of the matter, you will break free from anger's seductive grasp.

Chapter 16

The realm of human emotions is a vast territory inhabited by centuries of wisdom and insights from scientists, psychologists, philosophers, and poets.

These luminaries have bestowed upon us countless theories and strategies to understand and navigate the labyrinth of our feelings, especially those pesky, negative ones.

Here's the catch though: most of what they've given us is, well, bullshit.

Beneath the surface of our anger and other negative emotions lies a tangled web of misconceptions, half-truths, and outright falsehoods. In other words, our emotions are usually caused by deeply hidden bullshit (wrongness and bad life philosophies).

Our challenge is made even more complex and confusing by the additional untruths, half-truths, and commonly accepted idiocies about what it means to be human and to FEEL HUMAN EMOTIONS.

One purpose of this book is to unveil and dismantle the majority of this "bullshit," particularly concerning our understanding of human anger.

Beneath the surface of our anger and other negative emotions lies a tangled web of misconceptions, half-truths, and outright falsehoods.

This chapter explores a fresh and more helpful perspective on anger that begins with a concept familiar to many: "programming."

Programming: The Unseen Internal Generator of Emotions

The concept of programming is neither new nor controversial. We've all heard of Pavlovian conditioning and how it molds the behavior of rats, dogs, and even circus elephants.

We also know humans can be programmed through education, religion, advertising, or content on social media platforms.

It's a biological reality. Our brains and bodies are in a perpetual state of programming from conception, shaping what we think, believe, and consider to be true.

Programming is the invisible hand that guides our daily existence. Human emotions are also subject to this programming.

Imagine yourself in front of a computer with a screen and a standard keyboard. When you press the "A" key, the letter "A" instantly appears on the screen.

If I asked you to explain why this happened, you'd likely say, "It happened because I pushed the 'A' key on the keyboard."

Yes, but if I asked you whether other factors were involved, you might realize hidden programs in the computer's background had to be present to create this outcome.

An operating system must be running in the background of the computer for the device to do anything. In addition, another program, like a word processor, must also be running, causing the computer to display the letter "A" when you press the A key.

What happens if these background programs are removed? Would the letter "A" still appear on the screen? No.

The outcome depends on programs that are not visible to the end user but are essential.

There are two key learnings to take away from this computer analogy:

1. These internal computer programs running in the background are invisible to us as users.

2. We needn't understand the intricacies of these programs, their construction, or the programming language behind them, to achieve our goal of displaying the letter "A."

Unless we're computer builders or programmers, most of us can blissfully ignore this hidden layer of "invisible" programming. It's irrelevant to our daily lives, and we usually forget it exists.

The Genesis of Human Emotions

Let's use this programming analogy to better understand our emotions. Picture them as emerging—within your brain and body—just as computer screens and keyboards function.

We are not mechanical devices like computers, but our emotions manifest like we are biological machines subjected to fundamental laws of programming.

When someone pushes your "A" key (triggering you to react with anger), and you feel the surge of this emotion in your body, *invisible programs in your brain and body are orchestrating your emotional experience.*

You are usually unaware of these internal programs. Most of us haven't been taught how they work or that they are even there.

However, they must be there for you to experience the emotion (all human emotions work this way, not just anger).

Some experts argue that we have core emotions fully developed at birth, like a dog's instinctual response to snarl when you try to take its bone away.

But unlike animals, our emotional responses are more complex and shaped by language and social conditioning as we grow.

Human emotions, in contrast to animal emotions, are socially programmed, and this is what underpins our emotional reactions, even though we can't witness our internal programs in action.

We are not mechanical devices like computers, but our emotions manifest like we are biological machines subjected to fundamental laws of programming.

Understanding human emotions begins with the concept of programming. In the next chapter, we'll discuss another crucial idea: automaticity.

This concept shows you what you can and can't control about your emotions and how to use that knowledge to your benefit.

Chapter 17

Automaticity is the tendency to operate on "autopilot." That is, to act effortlessly and without conscious thought.

Think back to when you drove to a destination, and when you got there, you barely recalled the journey. That's automaticity at work.

Or consider the skill of typing, where your fingers dance across the keyboard, without a single conscious thought about tapping each letter, as I am doing right now. This is a true testament to the power of automaticity.

Even those times when you've instinctively reached a conclusion, snatched a falling object, or smashed a curveball out of the park— it's all thanks to automaticity.

In the realms of psychology and neuroscience, this concept isn't new or controversial. It's widely accepted as a fundamental aspect of our human nature, and people have been discussing it for centuries.

In 2011, the esteemed Princeton Professor of Psychology and Nobel Prize Winner in Economics, Daniel Kahneman, shed more light on this idea in his New York Times bestseller, "Thinking, Fast and Slow."

Kahneman reveals that our thinking is driven by two primary systems:

- System 1, which is fast, intuitive, and emotional (the essence of emotions is automaticity), and

- System 2, which is slower, more deliberate, and logical and rational.

Both systems coexist within us, sometimes vying for control.

We perceive ourselves as predominantly functioning in System 2 (reason and rationality), but Kahneman's research suggests that most of the time, we're operating in automatic thinking mode (System 1).

Human automaticity occurs in two forms. First, some biological functions, like breathing and the heartbeat, operate autonomously. Hormonal cycles and daily rhythms like the circadian and monthly menstrual cycles also tick away without conscious intervention.

Second, we operate automatically due to our programming. When you first learned to ride a bike or drive a car, those intricate movements weren't hardwired into your brain and body. Your brain and body eventually became programmed with practice, allowing you to perform these actions effortlessly and automatically.

Emotions, too, emerge through programming and automaticity.

Something triggers your brain and body, activating pre-established programs that release specific hormones and neurotransmitters, giving rise to what we call emotions.

This process unfolds so rapidly and reflexively that it circumvents rational thinking.

Here's the crux of automaticity:

--YOU do not think or perceive your emotions into existence.

--YOUR BRAIN and BODY (brain-body) think and perceive your emotions into existence instantly, based on the specific ways your brain-body has been programmed.

This is how your emotions typically come to be.

Sure, you can intentionally summon an emotional state by thinking about sad, scary, or anger-inducing things. But most of the time, emotions emerge automatically, in knee-jerk instantaneous fashion, shaped by our conditioning.

Now, we talk about controlling our emotions, but let's be honest—most of that talk is nonsense. Given what we've just explored about programming and automaticity, you'll understand we have limited control over the emergence of our emotions.

We get triggered, our pre-conditioned brain-body reacts, and emotions automatically follow.

Here's the good news: You do have control over what you think and do once you notice you are emotionally triggered.

Both systems coexist within us, sometimes vying for control.

In other words, channeling Kahneman, you can switch from System 1 (automatic thinking/reacting) to System 2 (deliberate/reasoned thinking/responding).

In subsequent chapters, you'll learn *precisely what's been triggered* inside you whenever you experience anger.

The tough news is that even though you will come to know and understand this emotion-generating mechanism, you won't be able to stop your triggered internal programs from automatically making you angry, at least in the short run.

Your triggered anger will still keep happening. But all hope isn't lost.

Once you grasp the specific internal programs producing your anger, you can address and negate your internal programming. Yes, you have the power to do this, and you can make this choice.

Picture yourself not as a single entity inhabiting your body—but as two beings coexisting inside.

One is the automatic, fast-reacting part of you, akin to Kahneman's System 1.

The other is a separate part capable of independent choices and intentional decisions, similar to Kahneman's System 2.

Emotional thinking and feeling comes from fast, automatic, System 1 thinking—right where it belongs. Emotions are frequently generated by automaticity.

With these two building blocks for understanding human emotions—**programming** and **automaticity**—we can now gain a clearer view of the emotional triggering process that has been going on for humans since the dawn of civilization.

However, our understanding of this process has been riddled with misconceptions for centuries. In fact, you could say it's been full of, well, let's call it—bull.

Chapter 18

D o you ever wonder if you have common sense?

Most of us believe we do. Yet, even if you're among the top 10% in the world who pride themselves on having common sense, you still face a significant challenge.

That's because COMMON SENSE OFTEN LEADS US ASTRAY!

Let's consider examples where common sense has stumbled.

Once upon a time, we were sure the Earth was flat, yet as we now know, it is round-ish.

We used to believe the sun rose in the morning and set in the evening. But, our planet is engaged in a daily dance of rotation.

In days gone by, we believed time and distance were constant, irrespective of our location in the universe or our speed of travel. Einstein unveiled the fallacy in this reasoning.

Speaking of Einstein, there was also a time when we thought matter and energy occupied separate realms and were two different things. Einstein shattered that illusion with his iconic equation, $E=MC^2$.

And remember, not too long ago, we thought Pluto was a planet.

The Root of Our Misjudgments

One of the main reasons common sense fumbles is its reliance on visibility.

We see the sun rising and setting; however, we don't see or sense the Earth's gradual spin beneath our feet.

Most of our cause-effect theories are overly simplistic (i.e., bullshit) because they are built mainly upon observable phenomena and their apparent interactions.

For example, we fire an arrow at an inflated balloon. When it punctures the target, we witness the balloon's disintegration right before our eyes.

Our brains promptly attribute the event to the arrow's impact. Our simplistic "1 directly causes 2" cause-effect theory would be correct in this situation.

Yet, when we examine human emotions and explore why certain events trigger them, common sense abandons us. Intelligence and education matter little in these moments.

Remember my story about running? I was a highly trained physician with a solid education. My common sense insisted running was a painful pursuit and the idea of running a marathon was definitely absurd.

My highly educated common sense told me quite clearly that I could never do it and could never possibly enjoy it.

Was my common sense understanding of running and my ability to enjoy it correct?

No. It was totally mistaken, and that realization only dawned on me years later.

Similarly, when I struggled with anger in my twenties and early thirties, common sense told me I would remain that way forever, and there was "no hidden anger champion within me."

Was common sense correct? Clearly not, or you wouldn't be reading these words today.

Ultimately, I discovered how to conquer anger by acquiring the insights I'm sharing with you here. One of the most profound was the realization our commonsense notions about the origins of our anger are fundamentally flawed.

Most of our cause-effect theories are overly simplistic (i.e., bullshit) because they are built mainly upon observable phenomena and their apparent interactions.

It was like the belief in a flat Earth or the pre-Einsteinian worldview, far removed from correct understanding.

So, what does common sense predict when it comes to the causes of anger?

Common sense predicts that something PUSHES OUR ANGER BUTTON (the metaphorical "A" key). This immediately and directly TRIGGERS THE SENSATION OF ANGER within us, as if it were simple and direct, "1 causes 2" cause-effect process.

I now know this simplified 1-2 "events-directly-cause-our-emotions" theory of anger is unequivocal BULLSHIT, and I invite you to see it the same way.

In the next chapter, I will show you what really stirs your anger.

Earlier, I described invisible programming deep within us, concealed from casual observation. But if you want to become a skilled anger eliminator, a high-level overview won't suffice; we need to dig deeper into the details of this programming and the inner workings of how anger is created.

Chapter 19

Anger Is a 1-2-3-4 (Cause-Cause-Cause-Effect) Process

H ave you ever been near someone with a cold or the flu, only to find yourself sick in a day or two?

For centuries, this baffled doctors and seemed like a mystery. Eventually, we discovered "invisible" agents like bacteria and viruses, and our understanding of infectious disease transmission deepened.

Later, we discovered another invisible factor—our body's immune system—and our comprehension expanded even further.

The same process of expanded awareness and knowledge is happening for human emotions.

*NOTE: I recommend the book **How Emotions Are Made** by Lisa Feldman Barrett for the best current brain science and detailed insights about human emotions.*

An Improved Way to Think About Your Emotions

For infectious disease transmission, we now have a simplified 4-part model for how viruses like the flu and the common cold propagate from one person to another:

1-------------[2]----------------[3]--------------4

In this model, A represents the initial sick individual, [B] represents the unseen virus, [C] represents the equally unseen functioning of your immune system—sometimes shielding you from illness—and D is the outcome, where you find yourself unwell due to a transmitted infection.

NOTE: [B] and [C] are shown in brackets to indicate they are invisible but still are critical parts of the process.

A comparable, 4-part sequence unfolds when we experience positive or negative emotions, such as anger:

A--------------[B]----------------[C]--------------D

Here, 1 represents the triggering event; [2] represents emotion-generating internal programs triggered within us; [3] represents another invisible internal process we haven't discussed yet; and 4 marks the outcome of this emotion-generating chain reaction, which in our example here, is anger.

The challenge for most of us is that steps [2] and [3] are totally concealed.

Not only are they invisible, but you also can't feel these two stages happening inside you, and you don't know how they work without proper training.

When it comes to comprehending our human emotions, MOST OF US REMAIN ENTIRELY UNAWARE that steps [2] and [3] even exist!

If you randomly ask people on the street, anywhere in the world, whether anger is a two-step or a four-step process, they would always respond with "2" because that's all we ever see or experience!

This is how misunderstandings (i.e., bullshit) spread far and wide. It's like the mistaken belief the sun is rising or setting when, in fact, the Earth is actually rotating.

The challenge for most of us is that steps [2] and [3] are totally concealed.

When I grappled with anger that seemed insurmountable forty years ago, I believed anger (and other emotions) were generated through a straightforward, 1-2 cause-effect process.

It wasn't until I realized emotions always arise from a 4-step causal process (cause-cause-cause-effect) that I began to search for and identify steps [2] and [3].

With those invisible puzzle pieces finally in my grasp, I unraveled the mystery of my anger and was able to leave my anger issues behind for good.

The point of this chapter? You can't easily find what is invisible, even if it's essential to your health and well-being.

You also can't begin to search for and uncover the hidden causes of your anger as long as you don't know what to look for.

The good news is once you understand this problem, you can get guidance (which this book provides) to conduct the hunt and capture your prize.

What is the essence of parts [2] and [3] of the anger creation chain?

We'll start with describing part [2] in the next chapter. There, I will introduce you to the critical concept of FILTERING, which is crucial for understanding where your anger really comes from.

Chapter 20

"To err is human…" Alexander Pope (1688-1744)

Let's dive into why I've labeled anger "the bullshit emotion." You might think it's because of all the misconceptions we've explored so far, and you're partly right.

But let's turn to something more profound: how anger, this age-old emotion humans have grappled with since the dawn of time, is rooted in what I call "filtered reality." Trust me, this is no exaggeration.

Where Did It All Begin?

The story of filtering goes back millions of years. As Homo sapiens evolved, our brains faced an overwhelming flood of information from the world around us.

There were genuine threats and dangers lurking at every turn, making it impossible for our tiny three-pound brains to process everything.

So, we had to adapt. Our brains developed shortcuts—they began to filter the endless stream of data into more manageable "chunks" to help us make quick decisions and survive.

This is where the phenomenon of "HUMAN FILTERING" was born.

The story of filtering goes back millions of years.

We don't perceive the world as it truly is; we experience it through multiple internal filters.

We don't see, feel, or experience this internal filtering process, but it goes on constantly.

Each of us has our own unique set of internal filters, and on an individual level, the filters that shape your reality are not the same as mine.

However, on a macro level, we share many similar filters ingrained in us through social conditioning.

Our views on "right" and "wrong" or "good" and "bad" are heavily influenced by societal norms. Just consider acts like chopping off heads and human sacrifices, which were once seen as "good" and are now universally regarded as "bad."

A bedrock principle is this: the reality you perceive is ALWAYS FILTERED REALITY.

This is why we all fall prey to different types of bullshit, regardless of our intelligence or education.

Our brains are constantly reducing a complex, multidimensional world into simpler thoughts and perceptions. In the process, OUR BRAINS ARE ALWAYS LEAVING THINGS OUT.

This is also why the old saying "to err is human" has held throughout history.

Filtering Produces Bullshit (Always)

This undeniable part of our existence is worth repeating. The dawn of human bullshit arose biologically from our filtering process. Thus, bullshit is not optional—it's an essential part of being human.

Once again, when your brain filters incoming data from the outside world, it inherently leaves things out.

The same thing happens when you focus on something specific that's of interest or importance; you inevitably disregard almost everything else in your environment.

For example, when I was in the early stages of learning to play tennis, my goal was to incorporate new athletic movements to improve my game. My coach would often tell me to focus intently on one aspect of my stroke. When I did this, as instructed, I would invariably forget to do other things that I'd previously learned.

Our brains can only take in part of life's intricate, multifaceted, multidimensional chess board all at once; they're always omitting details.

In other words, our brains generate bullshit constantly!

---

bullshit is not optional—it's an essential part of being human.

To make matters worse, our brains can also conjure up things that aren't really there—they can filter things in, not just filter things out.

As a result, everything we perceive is FILTERED REALITY. As such, our perceptions are routinely susceptible to both ERROR AND DISTORTION.

If you look deeply into your personal views of "truth" and "reality" with a commitment to radical honesty, you'll uncover layers of bullshit you adopted unknowingly.

Even if you remain unaware of your bullshit, the bullshit is still there, causing mischief (and anger) in your life.

Chapter 21

L et's take a moment to recap what you know or should be able to assume so far:

- Emotions don't just spontaneously erupt from external events; they're born from internal processes we can neither see nor sense.

- These processes are guided by our internal filters—shaping our perceptions, thoughts, and beliefs.

- These filters are a result of our lifelong conditioning and societal influences (along with genetic predispositions).

- Once established, these filters trigger automatically in response to various real or imagined stimuli.

- You can't easily stop or control your automatic filtering and the emotional reactivity it sometimes produces (more on this later).

- Changing your internal filters isn't a simple task (not discussed so far, but remember these filters have become ingrained into your brain, body and nervous system).

- Another internal source of emotions, represented by step [3] in our anger-producing chain, still lurks in the shadows (more on that in Chapter 23).

- When you get emotionally charged, especially with anger, your most potent tool is to **pinpoint the exact filters operating within**

you. Then, closely examine the resulting perceptions, thoughts, and beliefs to check their veracity (more on this is coming up).

• Anyone with an average IQ and a functional brain can identify the internal filters that fuel everyday emotions and assess whether they align with reality.

• Whether you believe you have this ability is irrelevant; it's an inherent ability inside each of us, ready to be unlocked with a small amount of training.

• Anger isn't a one-size-fits-all emotion; it can range from minor irritations to explosive fury.

• Each individual experiences anger differently, with varying levels of awareness and intensity.

I'm not claiming to have a perfect model for how our emotions get generated inside our brains and bodies. I am also not claiming to know the absolute truth about human emotions.

It's my belief, however, from personal experience and working with hundreds of clients, that the model for understanding human emotions presented in this book will serve you very well.

With the Anger Internal Causes Framework (explained in this chapter and the next) combined with the Ultimate Anger Elimination System described later in this book, you will gain immense personal power and control over your emotions.

Personally, I will employ any reliable system or method to master my emotions effectively, whether it's entirely correct or not. I invite you to embrace this same pragmatic, results-oriented philosophy, too.

The Three Cognitive/Perceptual Filters That Fan the Flames of Human Anger

You are about to learn something very powerful that most people don't know or appreciate about their own feelings of anger.

Anyone with an average IQ and a functional brain can identify the internal filters that fuel everyday emotions and assess whether they align with reality.

Here are the internal filters responsible for generating your anger— universal filters that affect all humanity.

These filters ignite your anger and the anger experienced by those around you. The same filters ignite anger in people across continents, cultures, and centuries. They will continue to do so for ages to come.

Without these **three specific lenses** through which we perceive the world, anger cannot exist. It's as straightforward as that.

The good news is, if you're harboring anger in any form, *you can instantly know the exact filters operating within you—even though you can't see them.*

To review, we are looking at anger (and all human emotions) as a four-step (cause-cause-cause-effect) process or model:

1----------------[2]------------------[3]------------------4

Where 1 is some precipitating or triggering event, [2] is how we think about, perceive, and experience that event through our internal filters, [3] is another yet-to-be-defined invisible internal process, and 4 is the result of the entire sequence, the anger we viscerally feel and sometimes express.

In this model, parts [2] and [3] are again shown in brackets to show these two steps are invisible.

In this chapter, we are starting on step [2]. To serve you best, we will break this second invisible step into two parts and cover step [2a]—the cognitive/perceptual filters that cause our anger to occur.

In the next chapter, we will examine the other part of this step [2b]. These are the behaviors that intensify and prolong our angry feelings.

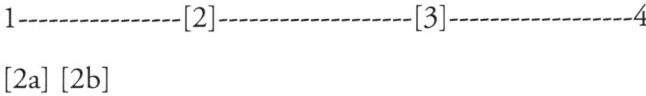

1---------------[2]------------------[3]-----------------4

[2a] [2b]

The Three Primary Internal Causes Of Anger

There are **three primary filters** responsible for all human anger, plus a fourth filter I'll unveil later in this chapter.

These first three filters are essential, required, and non-negotiable, while the fourth is an optional add-on (plus 1).

They are the specific automatic ways we perceive and think about events that generate the emotion of anger.

Here are the three primary filters:

1. Someone or something did something "bad" or "wrong" they shouldn't have done.

It's rare for anger to surface when acts appear wonderful, generous, loving, or "right."

2. Someone or something suffered harm, humiliation, embarrassment, offense, disappointment, inconvenience, or other negative consequences due to the actions taken.

We also tend not to get angry when something bad happens, but nobody gets hurt, like the saying "no harm, no foul."

3. The entity responsible for the "bad" or "wrong" action, which caused harm or negative consequences, bears 100% of the blame (unilateral blame) for both #1 and #2 above.

In simpler terms, anger stems from instinctively and automatically viewing certain life events through these three internal filters:

1. Someone/something did what they/it shouldn't have done.

2. Someone/something suffered negative consequences.

3. The someone/something is entirely to blame.

Without these three specific lenses through which we perceive the world,

anger cannot exist.

A Few Illustrations

Consider the 9/11/2001 TV images you saw where two separate planes struck the adjacent World Trade Center buildings in New York, resulting in thousands of casualties. If you felt anger when you saw these images or experienced the event in person, why did this emotion occur?

Here's how this event fits the Anger Internal Causes Framework:

1. The hijackers committed a horrendous act they shouldn't have done.

2. American citizens (and others) were grievously harmed.

3. The hijackers bear full responsibility for their actions and the ensuing harm.

As another example, imagine you're in a grocery store and witness a mother slapping her unruly child. If this incites anger in you, it's due to a specific set of thoughts and perceptions activated inside you:

1. The mother acted inappropriately by slapping her child.

2. The child endured harm (the slap) and potential long-term damage.

3. The mother is entirely responsible for choosing to slap her child.

And here's a third example: on March 27, 2022, during the televised Academy Awards show, comedian Chris Rock made a joke about actor Will Smith's wife, Jada Pinkett Smith, who was also in the theater audience.

Will Smith immediately became angry, got out of his seat, walked up onto the stage, and responded by slapping Chris Rock in the face.

Here's how Will Smith must have viewed the situation in order to get so angry:

1. Will saw Chris Rock making an inappropriate joke about his wife.

2. Will believed he and his wife were negatively impacted by the joke and possibly also publicly embarrassed because it aired on national television.

3. Will held Chris Rock 100% accountable (unilaterally to blame) for his actions—choosing to tell that joke.

Take any example of anger from your own life, and you'll find it neatly aligns with this **three-filter framework.**

If you come across an example that appears not to fit, take some time to think about it. Eventually, it'll conform.

The Fourth Anger Filter (Plus 1)

There's a fourth anger filter that many of us have. Unlike the first three filters, this one isn't a primary cause of anger. It's more of a societal expectation, and its strength varies across cultures and societies.

This fourth filter can be summed up as follows: If someone commits a wrongful act, causes harm, and is wholly or primarily responsible, we expect them to:

4. Acknowledge their wrongdoing, offer to make amends, and sometimes face consequences or punishment.

This expectation is particularly robust in American society and is embedded in our legal system's approach to punishing crimes. When this expectation is violated, our anger intensifies.

Have you ever witnessed someone, whether a friend or a stranger, committing a wrongful act that harmed another, and you believed they were entirely to blame? And suppose you confronted them, only to have them refuse to admit fault?

This refusal likely heightened your anger. Here's why:

1. Their refusal to admit wrongdoing and take responsibility becomes another wrongful act (second major wrongdoing) in your eyes.

2. You experience disappointment and distress over their refusal, causing further negative impact.

3. You view the person as 100% responsible (to blame) for not owning up to their actions.

It's a second helping of anger layered atop the initial offense.

Your Toolbox

You now understand the three primary (plus one additional) internal causes—cognitive and perceptual filters—that underlie all human anger.

Though few understand their nature, these filters are ingrained in all of us.

By reading this book, you now know what these anger-producing filters are.

They are the same filters producing anger in human beings for thousands of years.

The good news is that with just a little bit of practice and repetition, you can now commit these filters to memory.

From this point onward, *you'll always be clear about the internal causes of your anger.*

You'll also comprehend why anyone else, regardless of the triggering circumstances, experiences anger.

Let me be clear—**the framework you just learned for pinpointing the internal causes of your anger (first three filters) will serve you well for the rest of your life.**

I've been using it to my benefit, and to benefit others, for over forty years, and I don't expect it to ever change or lose its value.

Are these the sole internal filters contributing to the emotion of anger? Probably not.

Is this the only model for comprehending the genesis of human anger? Certainly not.

Numerous experts have proposed alternative theories and frameworks for understanding and theorizing why humans become angry.

Yet, in this book, I am giving you a framework (and a system that works with it) that has been exceedingly valuable and transformative for me and many others.

If you find alternative perspectives and methods for understanding and dealing with anger, and they grant you the power to swiftly quell anger when needed, by all means, embrace them.

My promise to you is that, as you progress through this book, you will discover that my approach to understanding the internal causes of your anger (Anger Internal Causes Framework) and my system to think and see beyond these causes (the Ultimate Anger Elimination System) will serve you exceptionally well and have a lasting and positive impact on your life.

Chapter 22

Have you ever wondered why anger can consume us longer than it should? Why anger sometimes lingers for weeks, months, years, or even generations?

The 90-Second Rule Of Emotions

The "90-second rule" is a term coined by Harvard brain scientist Dr. Jill Bolte Taylor in 2009.

Dr. Taylor's groundbreaking discovery revealed that when we experience an emotion like anger, a specific combination of hormones and neurotransmitters is released within our bodies. These chemical substances gradually rise to a peak and then return to their baseline values. Astonishingly, this entire process typically takes about just 90 seconds.

Dr. Taylor's profound insight is this:

Any emotion that persists beyond this 90-second window is not biologically normal. It means we are doing something to intensify or prolong that emotion unnecessarily.

In this chapter, you will learn the four most common ways we make feelings of anger more intense or prolonged than they need to be.

This is the second part of the invisible Step [2] in our four-step anger generation model—**[2b] internal action patterns.**

1----------------[2]------------------[3]-----------------4

[2a] [2b]

Let's first clarify a few key distinctions between cognitive/perceptual filters ([2a]) and internal action patterns ([2b]).

Unlike the cognitive/perceptual filters, which are **the primary internal causes** of our anger, the action patterns are not anger-initiating causes.

They are specific actions we either take or fail to take that can exacerbate our emotional turmoil once it has been generated.

For example, suppose you need to file your income tax returns and pay taxes owed to the federal government. But you don't file your returns.

In that case, this can lead to serious adverse consequences.

This is an instance of failing to take a necessary action, which in our framework still counts as an action pattern.

While the three primary cognitive/perceptual filters are always present when anger arises, the four action patterns are more variable.

Some episodes of anger may involve all four patterns, while others might only have one or two.

Thus, when it comes to action patterns, you must evaluate each situation individually to identify which, if any, are in play.

These four action patterns are not the only ones that can prolong or intensify anger.

For example, constantly ruminating about a triggering situation or replaying past anger-producing events in your mind are surefire ways to exceed the 90-second time limit, even though they aren't on our list of four.

Let's explore these four common action patterns that intensify and prolong our anger:

A. Failing to Acknowledge Differing Perspectives, Values, and Standards. One common pitfall is failing to recognize that our judgments, evaluations, and standards may not apply universally. When we label someone's actions as "bad" or "wrong," we often neglect to consider whether the behavior violates objective standards. In those moments of reflexive judgment, we might be clouded by our own biases, and our initial knee-jerk judgments may not be well founded.

B. Overlooking Our Role in the Situation This pattern links to the automatic perception someone else is 100% responsible or to blame for the action or actions that caused harm. When assigning blame, we tend to wear very narrow perceptual blinders and solely focus on the main perpetrator's behavior, neglecting other causes, including our actions.

For example, in long-term relationships, we subtly influence or contribute to the other person's problematic behaviors without realizing it. In such situations, accusing them of being solely responsible can be a form of self-deception (i.e., bullshit).

C. Justifying Our Anger When anger strikes, we feel justified in our emotional response. This initial justification prompts us to selectively search for further evidence and social agreement, reinforcing our anger and amplifying it rather than challenging its root causes (within us).

This causes us to ignore the possibility our anger is based on false assumptions or a distorted view of reality, opting instead to cling to our anger, defend it, and thereby prolong it.

D. Retaliation and Revenge The fourth action pattern corresponds to the expectation that individuals who do wrong should own up to their wrongdoing, make amends, or face punishment. When people escape consequences for their actions, we may take it upon ourselves to deliver justice.

In this retaliation mode, we've already justified our anger and are ready to exact revenge. The focus shifts from understanding the truth about our anger (and its internal causes) to imposing our penalties, leaving no room for self-reflection.

Actual personal growth and maturity involve acknowledging our potential for error, especially when we firmly believe we are right.

Accepting we may be wrong about many things, even when we're convinced of our righteousness, is a fundamental aspect of human growth and maturity. It is also the centerpiece of the anger elimination system recommended in this book.

When it comes to action patterns, you must evaluate each situation individually to identify which, if any, are in play.

Incorporating these additional insights about the invisible internal causes of our anger—[2a] and [2b]—puts the complete Anger Internal Causes Framework into your emotional toolbox, so you can gain greater control over your anger.

There's one more piece to our four-step anger-generation puzzle to fill in. To learn about the second invisible cause (Step [3]), please continue on to Chapter 23.

Chapter 23

The second hidden step in our four-step anger generation model—Step [3]—is the automatic, invisible, lightning-fast, incontrovertible "Stamp of Truth."

1----------------[2]-------------------[3]-----------------4

[2a] [2b]

This invisible step means that we automatically accept what our internal filters and action patterns serve up as truth, even though it is often distorted and inaccurate.

So there is a triggering event or occurrence (usually visible or otherwise sensed), which is perceived through your automatic invisible filters, and then your brain-body instantly and automatically "stamps" whatever comes through your internal filters as "truths" as opposed to filtered, often distorted internal realities. This is how anger (and other human emotions) arise from invisible processes within us.

When you find yourself engulfed in anger, have you ever wondered WHO exactly is thinking, perceiving, and behaving in ways that fuel your anger?

The answer might seem obvious at first—YOU.

But let's dig a little deeper and ask, what part of you is engaged in this anger-generating process?

In Chapter 17, we explored automaticity, which explains our answer. If by "YOU" you mean your conscious, reasoning self, then no, it is NOT "you."

Your automatic, previously conditioned self (I.e., your conditioned brain-body) takes the reins in these moments of emotional reactivity.

YOU, in the sense of your conscious, reasoning self, are merely a spectator on the sidelines.

When you get triggered into anger, your conditioned BRAIN-BODY, including all its intricate connections, becomes the active participant.

It calls the shots. It decides what to focus on and how to interpret and perceive the situation. It controls how it filters your "reality" through its established patterns and internal conditioning.

YOU receive the end result or output (Step 4—Anger) of this four-step anger generation process. But make no mistake, it's an invisible process that often churns out a lot of bullshit.

When you get triggered into anger, your conditioned BRAIN-BODY,

including all its intricate connections, becomes the active participant.

Remember, you always react emotionally according to your triggered internal filtered thoughts and perceptions, whether accurate or not.

The second invisible step, Step [3], occurs within your brain-body complex, as the last internal action before your emotions get produced.

Step [2a] alone isn't enough to produce your emotions; you must also BELIEVE in the accuracy of what your internal filters present to you. This is the job of Step [3].

Your BRAIN-BODY tells you that you must accept these filtered thoughts, perceptions, and behavioral responses as ABSOLUTE TRUTHS, not mere distortions or likely falsehoods (i.e., bullshit).

Your BRAIN-BODY's task is to make sure you believe whatever emerges from its filtering process is accepted by you as incontrovertibly true.

This happens instantaneously, at lightning-fast speed, and is incredibly difficult to notice and question.

Your BRAIN-BODY proclaims, "This is the truth, the whole truth, and nothing but the truth." Doubting or disagreeing seems either foolish or unthinkable.

This is why anger often arises from a foundation of bullshit.

The initial triggering event passes through the three cognitive/perceptual filters detailed in Chapter 21. The four action patterns explained in Chapter 22 can exacerbate or prolong it.

Then the automatic, invisible, lightening-fast, incontrovertible "stamp of truth" gives the final internal boost to your filtered "internal realities," by cementing them in your psyche, which gives them the final authority to create your anger.

The problem we all have as human beings is that often one or more of these filtered "internal realities" or reactive behavior patterns are flawed, incomplete, or significantly distorted.

However, after the automatic, invisible, lightening-fast, incontrovertible "Stamp Of Truth" is instantly applied, it is tough to notice this and take corrective measures.

This is why, when you try to use common sense to understand what's causing you to feel angry, your answers usually end up being bullshit.

It's bullshit because we typically overlook and leave out the two most important internal causes—Step [2] and Step [3].

To break free from this cycle and live a happier, anger-free life, you must make two significant changes that go against your automatic tendencies:

1. **Associate ANGER and BULLSHIT.** Start connecting your feelings of ANGER in your body with the word BULLSHIT in your mind.

Why would you do this?

Because in the real world, anger is usually generated by internal bullshit, but this truth is generally hidden from your view. Embrace this association, and you will gain a much deeper understanding of your emotional life (not just with anger, but for other emotions as well).

2. **Become a Truth Hunter.** Quickly shift into truth-hunting mode the moment you feel anger or notice it creeping in. Examine your filters and action patterns (you now know what they are) and hunt for the underlying truth beyond the BULLSHIT causing your anger to occur, just as you might hunt for a set of lost keys. Note: not all of your filters might be transmitting bullshit, but usually one or more of them are.

Once you've located the internal BULLSHIT responsible for your anger, which is now easy to do since it will always be what is coming in through Filters 1, 2, or 3, stretch yourself to hunt for deeper or less apparent truths (not so easy to do, at first).

Gather the truths you find and compare them to the BULLSHIT your BRAIN and BODY keep serving up to you.

By becoming a hunter-gatherer of truth, instead of the automatic recipient of filtered bullshit, you'll notice much of your anger will dissipate.

Over time, as you practice this approach, you might find that what once quickly infuriated you no longer holds any power over you. Your emotions and triggered reactions will slowly begin to change, once you see life more clearly and correctly, as opposed to the triggered "internal realities" that get activated inside you.

Contrary to popular belief, it's possible to make your anger vanish whenever you want. All you have to do is embrace the equation

ANGER = BULLSHIT and then search for the truth that your internal filters and action patterns are concealing from you.

By becoming a hunter-gatherer of truth, instead of the automatic recipient of filtered bullshit, you'll notice much of your anger will dissipate.

In the end, this book is a powerful guide to help you see through the hidden bullshit that is causing your anger to occur, and then discover a path to a more peaceful and happy life.

Chapter 24

Why Most of Our Anger (95%) Comes From Internally-Generated "Fake News" (In Other Words...Bullshit)

A s you read the previous chapter, did you get a sense of déjà vu? You know, that feeling of watching a familiar scene or series of events play out right before your eyes?

If so, there's a good reason that happened.

The process that occurs inside our brains and bodies that orchestrates the symphony of our emotions, including the storm of anger, bears an uncanny resemblance to the way our favorite media outlets behave.

In other words, our brains and bodies function much like our own personal news sources, constantly churning out fake stories and narratives for us to consume and believe in.

It's crucial to understand that all news in the media, whether it leans right, left, or anywhere in between, is FAKE NEWS.

Some outlets may serve up more fake news than others. Still, they all share one thing in common: each one heavily filters information before delivering it to us.

Why, you ask, is all news from the media fake news?

Because every news piece is filtered news, just like our internal thoughts and perceptions are always filtered "realities."

No news source can provide you with events precisely as they transpired. There's simply too much happening to cover every detail or potential story, and that's where filtering comes into play.

Our brains have grappled with the same dilemma for millions of years. The vast ocean of information and events outside of us is too much for our brains to capture and process. Hence, the need for filtering.

Any newsworthy event a media outlet selects to report on always undergoes one or more human observer's interpretations, further condensing, editing, distorting, and spinning the narrative.

And that's not considering the selection process itself (also filtering), which leaves out many important current events.

The process that occurs inside our brains and bodies that orchestrates the symphony of our emotions, including the storm of anger, bears an uncanny resemblance to the way our favorite media outlets behave.

When news from media sources reaches your eyes or ears, it's undergone significant alterations from its original state. It's been converted into a form of BULLSHIT to varying degrees.

Deep down, we all grasp this reality and have come to accept it.

What might be less apparent, though, is that our own BRAINS and BODIES generate just as much fake news as the most biased news agencies.

It's our internal FAKE NEWS that serves as the primary driver of most of our anger.

Internal FAKE NEWS (filtered reality) is also the driving force behind all our other positive and negative emotions.

Remember those moments of blind infatuation during the early stages of romantic love? Did your BRAIN and BODY offer you accurate information about the object of your affection, or did you later discover it was at least partially FAKE NEWS?

Our internal FAKE NEWS can also lead to relationship failures and divorce, as we often operate under misconceptions about how relationships truly function.

The same FAKE NEWS gnaws away at our self-worth and innate talents and, tragically, sometimes leads to acts of self-harm or suicide.

And here's a big revelation: both our internal and external FAKE NEWS sources also prevent us from realizing we can eliminate anger anytime we want.

We all have the ability to do this. We just need the proper framework for understanding its internal causes (see Chapters 21, 22, 23) and an effective SYSTEM for addressing these root causes once we know what they are (coming soon).

This is why anger is essentially a byproduct of BULLSHIT— multiple kinds and at numerous different levels.

Have you ever noticed how news outlets are remarkably adept at stoking your anger? Have you noticed they also can skillfully elicit fear, envy, guilt, and other potent emotions?

They've honed this ability because they are masters at creating and disseminating BULLSHIT.

They know BULLSHIT when they see it and create it, and they understand BULLSHIT is the fuel of human emotions.

Don't take my word for this. Look for yourself at how the genuine, world-class media BULLSHIT experts function every day.

They excel at understanding and provoking human emotions—because their business model depends on it—and they're well-versed in what's happening beneath the surface (inside us) where our emotions get generated.

They are expert at using this knowledge about how human emotions originate from bullshit, in order to make you feel however they want you to feel.

Chapter 25

I n 1989, the renowned psychotherapist and bestselling author Wayne Dyer published a book titled "You'll See It When You Believe It." The book surged into popular culture, celebrating the profound influence of visualization and positive beliefs.

Dyer's book is relevant because this chapter's primary theme is that you can **make anger vanish at will** without relying on conventional anger management techniques.

I understand you might be skeptical. You might think, "I won't believe that until I see it."

That's fine because seeing is believing. You may remain unconvinced until you experience anger's swift disappearance for yourself, employing the life changing Ultimate Anger Elimination System I reveal to you in this chapter.

In contrast to where you might stand on this point right now, I'm a true believer because I have benefitted from this system for over four decades and taught countless others to do the same.

I'm here to introduce this transformative system, knowing that if you embrace it, you'll come to appreciate its potential, meaning your potential as well.

Welcome to the Ultimate Anger Elimination System (S-C-C-S)

Unlike the conventional notions of expressing or suppressing anger (Chapter 5), I offer you a different approach that seems almost magical.

The "magic," however, arises from a powerful fundamental principle—**telling the truth**.

Since most of our anger stems from internally filtered "bullshit," often concealed from our awareness—the remedy for anger is telling the truth.

I uncovered this life-altering revelation more than forty years ago. Since then, I've harnessed its power for my benefit, finding tranquility and peace of mind that is hard to disturb.

Here's a condensed overview of the Ultimate System for Eliminating Anger. Employ this system anytime you recognize anger has been triggered within you in any of its forms—from mild annoyance or irritation to full-blown fury:

1. **CONFIRM.** Use the Anger Internal Causes Framework (Three primary cognitive/perceptual filters explained in Chapter 21) to **verify/confirm** you were thinking and perceiving in all three of these ways (if you are feeling angry, you have to be doing this);

2. **SUSPECT.** Remember the equation ANGER=BULLSHIT and **suspect** there is probably an error in one or more of your three primary filtered internal realities, even though they all might look and feel absolutely true to you because of the stamp of truth.

3. **SEARCH.** Based on your reasoned suspicion, begin to **search for errors or blind spots** and try to connect with deeper truths about whatever might have happened to trigger you;

4. **CORRECT.** As you discover errors/distortions/blind spots in your automatic filtered internal realities, and as you connect with what is more deeply true and accurate, make appropriate **corrections** in your thinking or actions.

I uncovered this life-altering revelation more than forty years ago. Since then, I've harnessed its power for my benefit, finding tranquility and peace of mind that is hard to disturb.

This may all seem pretty abstract, so I will give you an example to illustrate the process. Say you got triggered to become angry because you viewed your spouse's or friend's behavior as "bad" or "wrong," and your brain-body immediately stamped your feelings as true.

After **suspecting** some hidden bullshit and then **searching** for it, you discover you were unfairly or unjustly judging them based on your own personal preferences or standards.

Once you recognize this is what actually happened, and that they weren't truly doing anything "bad" or "wrong," you can then apologize, make amends, and/or promise to be more careful to avoid the same mistake in the future (even though there's a good chance you will automatically repeat it).

While this Ultimate Anger Elimination System seems simple, it's anything but easy to deploy.

Humans aren't naturally inclined toward truth-telling; we've grown accustomed to living with various shades of deception (bullshit) all around us.

Therefore, you must push yourself to see beyond your automatic perceptions, ingrained beliefs, and triggered "internal realities" to truly grasp this system's potential.

Let me illustrate with a personal anecdote from my life that mirrors the general example I cited above.

My wife and I have been married for nearly four decades, and we rarely experience anger in our relationship. However, early on in our marriage, there was one peculiar pattern where we'd argue when returning home from car trips. This rarity drew my attention, and I went on a search to uncover the source of our disputes (SUSPECT).

Here's how this pattern typically unfolded: I was usually behind the wheel as we drove back home from our trip. At some point, Christina would say, "Hey, there's something near here I'd like to see or visit, and it's only an hour off our path home."

My immediate response would be a firm, irritated "NO, we're NOT going to do that." This exchange would escalate into a heated argument, making the home-bound journey uncomfortably tense.

After several repetitions of this pattern, I SUSPECTED something deeper was at play. I donned my "BULLSHIT HUNTER" hat and began investigating the internal roots of my anger (SEARCH) after CONFIRMING that I was indeed angry because I was looking at my wife's behavior through the three primary anger-producing filters. After confirming the answers were: YES, YES, and YES, I started with the first cognitive/perceptual filter and asked myself the following question:

Question (to myself): Is it true that Christina is really doing something bad or wrong by suggesting a deviation from our intended route home?

Once I asked myself this question, to intentionally challenge my own internal reality, the answer quickly became clear—she wasn't wrong; she simply wanted to experience our journey home differently.

Our families had different traditions for driving home from vacations, and we each carried those experiences and expectations into our relationship.

My brain-body had been conditioned, through my family experiences as a child, to have me perceive her request as fundamentally wrong (which turned out to be BULLSHIT). I could now easily see through that falsehood without much effort to connect with a more profound truth—I was wrong for judging her so unfairly.

In this example, my anger was eliminated entirely just by examining and debunking the first cognitive/perceptual filter that was operating inside me.

I could also have examined and challenged the other two filters as well:

Question 2: Was I really negatively impacted by Christina wanting to deviate slightly from our direct path home? ANSWER: Not really. We had no reason to get home by a particular deadline. I only felt negatively impacted because I had an exaggerated need for her to do things my way.

Question 3: Was Christina totally responsible or to blame 100% for asking to deviate from our direct path home? ANSWER: Yes and No. Yes, in that she decided to ask, and I didn't do anything to trigger that request. And No, I usually took the lead in driving home and determining our route without involving her in the decision.

In this case, I successfully eliminated this recurring anger issue by recognizing a flaw in my first anger-producing internal filter and confronting the actual truth (CORRECTION).

Today, when we are driving to any destination, and Christina suggests a detour, if there is no good reason not to go there, my response is, "Sure, honey, whatever makes you happy."

I genuinely feel no upset now because I no longer perceive her request as fundamentally wrong (I CORRECTED MY MISTAKEN NEGATIVE JUDGMENT); I now see it more correctly as a legitimate desire that, as her partner and husband, I now strive to honor.

This example highlights how acknowledging your internal bullshit, seeking the truth, and taking corrective actions can dissolve persistent patterns of anger.

Humans aren't naturally inclined toward truth-telling; we've grown accustomed to living with various shades of deception (bullshit).

With decades of repeated practice, I've encountered countless other instances where my anger was coming from internal bullshit, and in each case, truth-telling extinguished my anger.

Once you clearly see the truth about any anger-triggering situation you've been involved in, it becomes difficult to unsee it. And the next time a similar or related incident triggers you, you can recall what you discovered to be true and use it again to your advantage.

I promise you, once you begin to experience the disappearance of your anger by embracing truth instead of remaining stuck in your automatic filtered bullshit, you'll become a believer like me, because you will see and feel the benefit, so you won't have to accept it just on faith.

In other words, you won't believe it until you see it…and until you feel it, by having your anger quickly disappear.

This approach works on all kinds of anger. It works on small types of anger like daily annoyances and irritations. It works on medium-sized anger. It even works on huge, rage-quality, hate your fellow neighbor type of anger.

I'm reminded of one publicized case of a young woman who was raised in a strong religious community that taught all their followers, from birth on, to view certain groups of people as evil, horrible individuals. This woman had bought into this philosophy and internalized it into her being. As a young girl, she even helped to lead passionate, hate-filled protests and demonstrations against these targeted groups.

Then, as she got older, she joined social media and started interacting clandestinely with some of these "horrible outcasts." She found out, through personal experience, they weren't nearly as bad as her elders believed. In fact, she discovered many of them were kind and caring, a lot like her.

Eventually, she realized that much of what she was taught, what she had dutifully internalized, and what drove her hatred for these groups, was not true at all. Her passion and hatred quickly disappeared, and she eventually left the religious community to pursue her life independent of all this hatred.

Remember, ANGER = BULLSHIT, and when the bullshit is revealed, the anger goes away. This is true even for extreme anger and hate, much like we are seeing all around the world.

Chapter 26

To switch to something a little less grim, let's talk about golf. Golf fascinates me. I'm an avid player and fan of the game.

If you've ever tuned in to watch professional golf on TV, you've likely witnessed a remarkable moment: a golfer raises their club to the top of the backswing, ready to deliver a powerful stroke, when suddenly, some unforeseen distraction intervenes, and the golfer abruptly halts their downswing right before completing the stroke to hit the ball.

Each time I witness this, I'm left in awe of the golfer's ability to achieve such a poised striking position, only to interrupt their swing in a split second. It always makes me wonder, "How on earth did they manage to do that?"

I want to share a story about when I was "stopping at the top of my backswing." Only it wasn't on a golf course; it occurred in my car, and the feat left me equally astounded...and quite pleased.

Out And About with My Daughter

Thirty years ago, on a quiet evening, I was out and about with Tracie, my four-year-old daughter. We were driving home, and she was securely strapped into her car seat, which was positioned in the middle of the back seat of my car. Suddenly, she whined and complained, "Daddy, I'm hungry."

I replied, "Tracie, we're almost home. Can't you wait a little longer?" Her response was immediate and insistent, "No, I can't wait; I need food now!"

We were near a fast-food restaurant, so I pulled into the drive-through and ordered a small bag of French fries and a drink, just as she asked. I handed her the food, expecting her to dig in and relieve her hunger. However, a few minutes later, when I glanced in my rearview to check on her, what I saw surprised and shocked me.

Instead of enjoying her meal, Tracie was taking the French fries out of the bag, breaking them in half, and placing them on the armrest of her car seat. To me, it appeared she was playing with her food, not eating it as I would have expected.

At that moment, anger began to boil within me. My internal filters and their rapid-fire "stamps of truth" went to work, convincing me she had deceived me by feigning extreme hunger, making her actions both wrong and manipulative.

I was irate, feeling negatively impacted, and totally abused. I was on the verge of turning my head and unleashing a torrent of parental anger upon her.

I was at the "top of my backswing" and about to "swing down" to release my fury.

A Pause That Made All the Difference

Then something remarkable happened. Just before letting my anger loose, I stopped and held my tongue.

Why? Because I had spent years scrutinizing my anger reactions in various situations and learned that, more often than not, I was somehow in the wrong (I SUSPECTED POSSIBLE BULLSHIT).

I decided to "abort my downswing" and allow Tracie to explain herself, even though I was sure her explanation wouldn't change my mind or diminish my anger.

I asked her, "Tracie, why aren't you eating your food?" Her response completely altered the moment. She calmly replied, "Daddy, the French fries are much too hot for me."

I immediately felt relieved and pleased I hadn't unleashed my anger upon her in a knee-jerk fashion. It dawned on me at that moment just how valuable all those years of training myself to associate anger with the likelihood of "bullshit" had been.

The Moral of This Story

I share this tale to illustrate how skewed our automatic "internal realities" can be. When you apply the Ultimate Anger Elimination System, which I introduced you to in the previous chapter, you must do so with an open mind and a commitment to uncovering the truth.

Begin with understanding why you got triggered to feel angry. You should now appreciate this is easy (CONFIRM the three primary filters explained in Chapter 21). In this instance, my brain and body distorted my perception of reality to make me believe:

1. My daughter had done something bad and wrong.

2. I had suffered negative consequences.

3. She was entirely responsible and to blame.

Simultaneously, my brain and body convinced me these internal perceptions were irrefutably true (STAMP OF TRUTH), leaving no room for questioning them or for considering alternative perspectives.

Fortunately, my pause allowed me to ask her for an explanation, and her response changed my viewpoint entirely. As I evaluated each of my internal causes of anger, in light of the new information I received from my daughter, I realized:

1. My daughter did nothing wrong by not immediately eating her food (TRUTH).

2. I hadn't been negatively impacted; she hadn't manipulated or tricked me (TRUTH).

3. She was still entirely responsible for her choices and actions, with me playing no role in her behavior. (At least this part was correct as initially perceived/filtered.)

I immediately felt...pleased I hadn't unleashed my anger upon her... It dawned on me...just how valuable all those years of training myself to associate anger with the likelihood of "bullshit" had been.

This is the essence of applying the Ultimate Anger Elimination System. You're always determining which of the three primary filters might be incorrect, incomplete, or misleading. Sometimes, only one is faulty; other times, it's two; occasionally, all three are off the rails.

In this instance, two out of three were wrong, and the third one was correct. Or at least that's what I thought.

Then Something Else Happened

There's an intriguing twist to this story. A few minutes later, as I continued driving home and my anger had entirely dissipated, I realized I had completely overlooked something.

Just two nights before this incident, Christina, Tracie, and I had dined at a local restaurant. Tracie ordered a child's meal with chicken tenders and French fries. As the waitress placed our plates on the table, I noticed hot steam rising from Tracie's French fries.

I immediately sprang from my seat to caution her against touching the hot fries. I broke them in half for her, one by one, a trick I learned as a child to cool them down quickly.

Believe it or not, I had completely forgotten I had done this two days earlier.

So in the end, not only had my daughter done nothing wrong, and not only had I not been taken advantage of, but I had also inadvertently taught her this behavior just two days prior—though I had completely forgotten about it.

So, she was not 100% responsible or to blame for her actions. As it turned out, the truth was that I, too, had a lot to do with it.

In retrospect, as I looked more closely and honestly at the internal causes of my anger in this situation, I realized I was three for three:

WRONG... WRONG... WRONG...BULLSHIT... BULLSHIT... BULLSHIT

You might assume such instances are rare, but they are not. Most of the time, when anger flares up, one or more of our three primary internal anger-causing filters will be wrong.

This means that most of the time if we really tell the truth, our anger will be coming from "bullshit."

Most of the time, when anger flares up, one or more of our three primary internal anger-causing filters will be wrong.

At this point, in case you didn't appreciate my earlier advice, you might want to take out a clean sheet of paper and start writing ANGER = BULLSHIT at least a hundred times.

You might even want to do this every day for a while, until you start seeing this life changing equation in your dreams.

This is the key to living and anger-free life. So don't rip yourself off by failing to do the work required to get there.

Part IV

From "Emotional Intelligence 2.0," Travis Bradberry and Jean Greaves, 2009

Emotions can help you and they can hurt you, but you have no say in the matter until you understand them.

We invite you to begin your journey now, because we know that emotional mastery and understanding can become realities for you.

The only way to genuinely understand your emotions is to spend enough time thinking through them to figure our where they come from and why they are there.

Chapter 27

I've been dedicated to teaching people the principles in this book for over four decades. If you embrace these ideas fully, you will deepen and broaden your understanding of human anger.

I've shared these insights in the past through online courses, seminars, workshops, and coaching programs. While some elements of this unique approach have appeared in my previous books, this comprehensive guide brings them all together. It greatly expands upon everything I've previously written about how to think about and deal with anger.

Over the past two years, I've made remarkable progress in reducing the time required for students to master the Anger Internal Causes Framework and the Ultimate Anger Elimination System.

The culmination of this work is my "Angry No More" ten-session coaching program, an opportunity for anyone to learn how to swiftly and effectively eliminate anger in just ten 1-hour Zoom sessions.

Pause for a moment and let that sink in. People who've battled anger issues for years, teetering on the edge of relationship breakdowns or health problems, have successfully learned to halt their anger in its tracks with just ten hours of training.

Why ten sessions and not twelve or twenty? Ten sessions provide ample time for most people to experience a complete turnaround in their ability to comprehend and consistently eliminate anger.

I've made remarkable progress in reducing the time required for students to master the Anger Internal Causes Framework and the Ultimate Anger Elimination System.

In the initial two sessions, I equip students with foundational knowledge about anger and the Anger Internal Causes Framework (discussed in Chapters 21, 22, and 23).

Then, in the subsequent eight sessions, we apply this framework and the Ultimate Anger Elimination System to real-life instances of anger they've encountered in the past or the present.

While I hope many of you will gain life-altering insights about eliminating anger just by reading this book and experimenting with the principles and strategies on your own, there's no substitute for working through your own personal experiences with challenging anger reactions.

In these deeply personal examples, you can practice telling the truth, transforming your relationship with anger, and honing your skills as an anger elimination master.

A book like this, or any other pre-structured learning format, can only provide so much. True mastery comes when you work through multiple anger issues as they arise in your life and as you reflect on your own past or recent experiences.

This is the most effective way to learn to eliminate anger.

If you're determined to put an end to your anger problems once and for all, I strongly recommend this path. Visit my website at http://DocOrman.com and use the contact tab to message me, and we can arrange a time to chat.

As far as I know, there is no other anger elimination program that can teach you to master your anger by recognizing and neutralizing its internal causes—in just ten sessions.

If you come across one, please let me know—I'd love to meet the creator and share our professional backgrounds and experiences.

In this part of the book (Part IV), I'll introduce a few people who have successfully completed my anger elimination coaching program and triumphed over anger, even when nothing else worked.

I'll also introduce you to five professional coaches and consultants who are beginning to incorporate the principles revealed here into their work with clients who grapple with anger issues.

In Parts V and VI, I'll continue offering practical tips and examples of how you can start implementing my Anger Internal Causes Framework and Ultimate Anger Elimination System.

With this knowledge, you can begin on your path toward increased happiness and better health, ensuring you don't end up in dire straits that lead to divorce and other heart-wrenching relationship breakdowns.

You don't have to look far to see the frequently encountered negative consequences of unchecked anger, which this book is designed to help you avoid.

Chapter 28

At a recent social gathering, amidst laughter and anecdotes, someone asked, "Have you ever heard what the letters 'RV' stand for?" I was intrigued; I had no idea. With a mischievous grin, the questioner revealed, "Ruined vacations."

The truth in those words struck me, because it fit one of my recent clients. Let me share the following RV story with you.

About two years ago, I received an urgent message from Frank. We had crossed paths briefly on a Florida golf course several months prior. We hadn't communicated since then, though he followed me on Facebook.

Frank explained he and his wife Ginny had recently returned from their first RV vacation, and his behavior had deeply troubled her during the trip.

He confided that his anger had been a constant irritant to his wife throughout the journey, straining their relationship. Concerned about this, Ginny urged him to seek help with his "anger issues."

We met the next day at a local ice cream shop, where cozy, shaded outdoor seating provided an ideal backdrop for our conversation.

Frank, a 66-year-old retired building inspector, had been married to his second wife, Ginny, for seven years. Their shared dream was to enjoy retirement by traveling the country in a used RV, which they had just purchased.

However, their inaugural RV trip had taken an unexpected turn. Inexperienced in piloting an RV, Frank found himself battling crosswinds and dealing with a series of malfunctions.

Frustration and irritation bubbled within him, and though none of it was directed at Ginny, she witnessed his incessant cursing, grousing, and fury from only a few feet away. When they returned home, Ginny confronted Frank, declaring she wouldn't take another RV trip with him until his anger was under control.

And thus, the urgent message to me. Frank was seeking help to salvage his marriage and his dreams of a carefree retirement.

As we discussed Frank's past, he revealed a childhood infested by anger within his family. He carried this emotional burden with him even though he distanced himself geographically.

He had managed to keep his anger under control for most of his life. Apart from basic anger management training, however, he hadn't taken any other steps to address the underlying issues.

Frank's age and lifetime of anger didn't deter me; I believed I could help him and told him so.

I shared the two critical insights that transformed my relationship with anger, which I revealed in Chapter 15. Here they are again for reference. When triggered by anything that causes anger, you're likely wrong about something or harboring a detrimental philosophy, or both.

Frank accepted the idea of exploring these two truths, and we started his ten-session program. In his initial two sessions, we covered the Anger Internal Causes Framework, explained in Chapters 21, 22, and 23.

Then, we applied this framework and the Ultimate Anger Elimination System—CONFIRM, SUSPECT, SEARCH, CORRECT—to real-life examples from Frank's life.

Ginny confronted Frank, declaring she wouldn't take another RV trip

with him until his anger was under control.

During each subsequent session, we scrutinized three to four anger episodes involving his wife, siblings, or reactions to current events. We even analyzed incidents like the altercation between Will Smith and Chris Rock, as well as his emotional response (intense anger) to Putin's military actions in Ukraine.

Through using the recommended framework and system, we identified unrealistic philosophies and other incorrect or distorted thinking and perceiving (filtering) that fueled his anger.

Between our weekly meetings, Frank diligently practiced using the Anger Internal Causes Framework on his own. Whenever anger surfaced, he referred to the three primary filters and practiced CONFIRMING his thinking and perceiving patterns.

He went a step further, applying this framework to TV shows he watched, repeatedly dissecting characters' angry emotions through the lens of the three primary filters.

By the fifth session, Ginny noticed positive changes. The minor irritations that once triggered Frank were losing their power.

By the eighth session, Frank's progress was undeniable. He no longer was plagued with angry outbursts on the golf course, a lifelong habit he'd struggled to break.

With my guidance, he had become proficient in using the framework and system independently.

Frank completed the ten sessions of my Angry No More program and graduated with newfound confidence, armed with tools to maintain his progress.

Several months later, he reported continued success. Ginny remained delighted with his improved demeanor, and they had enjoyed several RV trips together without anger-related incidents.

Frank's victory is a testament to the potential for change, even if you come from an angry family and have grappled with anger for decades.

With the proper framework and systematic approach, you can conquer anger and replace "ruined vacations" with "rekindled vacations."

Frank provided an endorsement for my program as he reflected on his journey:

"I am a happily married, retired man. My life was good, except I had a short fuse that made me very quick to anger.

Dr. Orman helped me recognize the root causes of my anger and taught me how to defuse them. Now, I feel much better and more in control of my emotions. My wife has seen significant changes in me, and I'm pleased about that, too."

At age 66, Frank's story is a reminder it's never too late to free yourself from the clutches of anger.

Chapter 29

Take a ride with me, back in time to three decades ago, when I was still engrossed in the practice of medicine. At that stage of my career, I offered a unique blend of services, including traditional medical care along with a few anger and stress counseling sessions each week.

One afternoon, my office manager penciled in a new counseling client, Jim, referred to me by one of his friends. When Jim arrived for his appointment, our first conversation was the beginning of a remarkable success story neither of us could have anticipated.

Jim was a 45-year-old entrepreneur, the proud owner of a small landscaping company. He was married with two teenagers. When he walked into my office that day, he wore the world's weight on his shoulders. His weary demeanor hinted at the ordeal he was about to describe.

His narrative painted a portrait of a man who had grappled with chronic anger and stress most of his adult life. His emotional turbulence was tied to the fortunes of his business. When the tides of commerce grew stormy, Jim's anger and stress levels surged, leaving a trail of turmoil that affected his employees and his family.

The last 6 months had taken an unprecedented toll on Jim. This time, it wasn't a downturn in business that was the source of his woes. Instead, an unexpected deluge of new clients and the accompanying demands for landscaping work overwhelmed his modest workforce.

Jim had made the bold move of hiring a new salesperson and two additional landscaping crews. Naturally, this expansion required his involvement in training and supervision on top of his other responsibilities.

As Jim took on this challenge, his anger and stress levels began to climb. He sought help from a prominent stress management psychologist in our area, dedicating three months to weekly sessions. But he saw no progress. This prompted the psychologist to suggest to Jim that he consult with a psychiatrist.

Though Jim had reservations about this next step, he heeded the professional opinion and advice. But after just two sessions, he received an unexpected and disheartening dismissal from the psychiatrist, who said, "I don't think you have what it takes to benefit from psychotherapy."

In a flash, Jim found himself back at square one, except now his emotional state had plummeted further into despair. Doubt weighed on his shoulders, casting a long shadow over his prospects for improvement.

In this dark hour, Jim confided in a few close friends, one of whom was acquainted with my work. This friend recommended he seek my help.

As I listened to Jim's tale of woe, I empathized with his plight. I had seen this pattern as a recurring theme among clients of mental health professionals entrenched in the conventional "stress management" and "anger management" mindsets.

Though I hadn't yet developed my groundbreaking Angry No More ten-session program, I was already conducting a more extensive stress mastery program heavily focused on eliminating anger.

I shared my conviction with Jim that there was hope despite his pessimism and history of fruitless efforts. I told him I could guide him to a better place if he put in the effort.

Jim's eyes, once clouded with doubt, sparkled with excitement. He readily jumped into my program.

He sought help from a prominent stress management psychologist...

but he saw no progress. This prompted the psychologist to suggest consulting a psychiatrist.

After just five one-hour sessions, he began to experience relief from his anger for the first time in memory. He embraced my framework and system for addressing the internal causes of his anger and started to see encouraging results.

Open and honest, Jim began to recognize how his own internal "bullshit" played a significant role in fueling his anger and other types of stress. This new perspective soon became a source of peacefulness and expanded confidence for him. Armed with this newfound clarity, he began to understand his inner dynamics better and discover how to take control.

After five more sessions, Jim's anger and overall stress levels receded even more. His workplace became more harmonious, and his family noticed a positive change in his demeanor at home.

I continued to counsel Jim for several more months until we both agreed he had made such remarkable progress that he was ready to navigate with my framework and system independently.

Our paths diverged after he graduated, and we lost touch. Twenty years later, our worlds collided at a local art show, and we took the opportunity to reconnect.

I asked Jim about his well-being and whether he still relied on my anger elimination framework and system.

His response filled me with awe. Jim continued to use these tools and had fully integrated them into his daily life. His wife and two now-grown children had repeatedly expressed gratitude for the permanent changes they had seen in him over time.

For a man once dismissed as "incurable" by two leading mental health professionals, I marveled at the lasting changes he easily achieved by embracing an approach that was vastly different from generally accepted anger and stress management principles.

...a man once dismissed as "incurable" by two leading mental health professionals...

Jim's story is a testament to the power of the right kind of guidance designed to produce lasting change.

Even in the face of seemingly insurmountable challenges, including the bullshit opinions of two highly respected professionals who could not see his true potential and inner power, Jim was able to connect with his inner anger champion and resolve his longstanding anger issues.

Chapter 30

P arenting a child with mental, emotional, or physical challenges can be an uphill battle that defies logic and pushes our boundaries. If you add being a single parent to the mix, the demands can become overwhelming.

In these situations, anger can quickly become a storm. This anger can sometimes escalate to a breaking point for a single mom like Kate.

Kate was a 40-year-old IT professional and a single mother of a 20-year-old daughter on the autism spectrum. While her daughter was high-functioning and mostly self-sufficient, there were moments when her behavior would test even the most patient of parents.

When her daughter misbehaved, Kate's anger surged uncontrollably, unleashing what she called her "rage attacks."

These highly emotional outbursts of screaming and yelling left her feeling terrible and burdened with guilt. Despite her best efforts, she couldn't find any way to end them.

She devoured countless books and articles on anger management and sought guidance from three different anger management experts, but her struggles persisted.

Then, Kate attended a virtual summit where I spoke about anger elimination. The prospect of something "new" and "different" intrigued her and offered hope where previous attempts had failed. Kate promptly arranged a consultation call.

During our Zoom conversation, I learned more about Kate's past history and current situation. I shared my belief I could assist her, and without hesitation, she enrolled in my *Angry No More* program.

During our first session, I introduced Kate to my framework for identifying the internal causes of her anger, which was entirely new to her.

She had never been told that there were hidden layers of unrecognized "bullshit" underlying her anger that were automatically coming from three anger-producing filters.

Kate diligently completed my ten-session Angry No More program and was astounded by the results. In her own words, she shared her experience:

"I'm a computer programmer and a single mom to an adult daughter with special needs. Anger was my constant companion and the reason I sought Dr. Orman s help. I tried counseling before, to no avail. I felt hopeless and feared I was going to remain an angry person for life, which would be bad for me and my daughter.

Dr. Orman introduced me to a new framework for understanding my anger and a system to eliminate my 'rage attacks.' In just a few weeks, my anger began to recede. My friends and family noticed a calmer version of me, and I found myself living a less stressful life.

One of the most profound revelations was recognizing my tendency to assume that explaining something once or twice to my special needs daughter would make it 'stick.' I assumed her brain functioned much like mine.

I came to realize, however, that her brain operated differently. Instead of seeing her actions as 'bad' or 'wrong' when she violated behavioral rules, I began to understand it was because of her unique way of processing information.

I also noticed how my own behavior contributed to some of her problematic actions. With this newfound awareness, I experimented with different approaches for disrupting these patterns, just like Dr. Orman did with his unconscious running habits."

Kate's journey shows that even intense, knee-jerk reactions of anger can be tamed or eradicated when we gain a deeper understanding of their concealed causes.

The previous anger management experts she consulted lacked these crucial insights, leaving her in the dark about what was causing her anger to emerge.

She had never been told that there were hidden layers of unrecognized "bullshit" underlying her anger...

To those professionals who come across this book, I invite you to embrace the principles explained herein and apply them in your work to improve the lives of those who turn to you for anger relief.

Together, with your existing commitment to help improve people's lives and the principles revealed in this book, we can unlock the path to lasting transformation, anger freedom, and reduced violence and hatred worldwide.

Chapter 31

I magine if the Emmy Awards had a category like "The Least Angry TV Producer"—wouldn't that be something?

While such an accolade doesn't exist, I had the privilege of sharing my Anger Internal Causes Framework and Ultimate Anger Elimination System with Rick, a distinguished three-time Emmy-winning TV producer.

Our paths had crossed at a speaking workshop in Texas. Rick, now retired from two decades in the television industry, was on hand to capture and professionally edit videos of me and the other speakers.

Our side conversations drifted toward my work and the unique approach I offered for tackling anger-related issues.

Intrigued, Rick asked more about my methodology and expressed a desire to explore it further. He confessed anger had once been a constant companion, especially during his years in television production.

After retiring, Rick had shed most of his anger tendencies. Now in a budding relationship with a new girlfriend, he was worried anger could resurface unexpectedly and damage his future romantic prospects.

Moreover, he carried some longstanding resentments related to his past divorce as well as lingering anger from other relationship breakdowns.

I taught Rick the Anger Internal Causes Framework, helping him gain fresh insights into the origins of his past and present anger.

We discussed minor irritations with his current girlfriend, revisited spousal anger episodes that ultimately led to divorce, and navigated through the anger he had experienced working for a large, bureaucratic corporate media company.

...he was worried anger could resurface unexpectedly and damage his future romantic prospects.

After our ten-session program, Rick was thrilled with his newfound knowledge and the power over anger it provided him.

Initially, he had hesitated to label himself an "angry person" because he didn't typically explode in fits of rage. However, he acknowledged he often felt irritation and annoyance and still carried unresolved anger from his past.

In his final session, Rick shared his thoughts with me on his experiences going through the program and the results he achieved:

• "I found your framework and system incredibly effective and appreciate how quickly it works."

• "Nearly everything you taught me was entirely new and eye-opening."

- "I was fully engaged in every weekly coaching session."

- "I now possess a much clearer and improved understanding of my anger."

- "If I had this knowledge about anger earlier in my life, it would have made a significant difference."

- "I used to get angry without understanding why, but now I can pinpoint the precise root causes."

- "I no longer search for external sources of my anger; I look within and find them there."

- "My confidence and control over my anger have greatly improved."

- "One major issue I had was forgiving myself for past actions; now, I can do so more truthfully and compassionately."

- "I realized I placed unrealistic expectations on past relationships and unfairly judged others for being different from my ideals."

- "Even my expectations about technology and video equipment have become apparent, making it harder for those expectations to catch me off guard now."

- "Living in LA, I used to experience anger on the roadways, but now I remain calm and composed even in bad traffic situations."

Today, Rick carries far less anger and resentment towards himself and others from his past. He's better equipped to nurture his current relationship without disruptive anger and radiates happiness and peacefulness, regardless of life's challenges.

Initially, he had hesitated to label himself an "angry person"

because he didn't typically explode in fits of rage.

However, he...often felt irritation and annoyance and still carried unresolved anger from his past.

Perhaps one day, Rick will produce a new documentary about my approach to anger elimination, and who knows, maybe a fourth major award might find its place on his bookshelf, alongside the three he's already earned.

Chapter 32

I n Wayne Dyer's book, "You'll See It When You Believe It," forgiveness is described as a process of correcting misperceptions we've woven with our thoughts. Once our thoughts become clear, forgiveness becomes less a practice and more a natural state of being.

Dyer emphasizes that believing others should not have treated us a certain way is the ultimate absurdity (bad philosophy). The universe unfolds as it should, even in moments we've deemed wrong, cruel, or painful. Instead of harboring anger at how we were treated, Dyer encourages us to view those actions differently, recognizing that people act based on the conditions of their own lives.

The universe unfolds as it should, even in moments we've

deemed wrong, cruel, or painful.

These words resonate with the core message of this book. If the roots of anger arise from bullshit, the path to freedom from anger and true forgiveness involves embracing the truth.

This brings to mind another client I worked with while I was still a practicing physician. Mark's story is one I shared in my 1991 award-winning book, "The 14 Day Stress Cure."

Mark, a 45-year-old man, sought my help because he harbored deep-seated anger toward both of his parents, even though his father had passed away.

As a young child, he was confined for over a year in a sanitarium due to rheumatic fever. His most painful memory was of his parents seemingly "abandoning" him at the sanitarium's doorstep. He also remembered that they rarely visited.

Even as an adult, Mark couldn't forgive what he perceived as such a huge parental betrayal.

After several counseling sessions, I encouraged Mark to investigate his assumptions by speaking with his elderly mother. He was to meet with her and ask her about her recollections of those prior events. He accepted this challenge, and the conversation brought about a profound and unexpected change in his long-held feelings.

Mark learned both of his parents were devastated by the decision to place him in the sanitarium. They only agreed under immense pressure from their family doctor, who believed it was the only way to save Mark's life.

Their guilt and despair were overwhelming, so much so that they could not bring themselves to witness their son's profound unhappiness, which they felt responsible for. So they rarely visited.

Mark realized his parents hadn't "betrayed" or "abandoned" him. Upon this realization, his heart swelled with compassion and empathy for their unbearable situation.

Mark's longstanding anger and resentment *vanished instantly*, and there was no need for forgiveness.

Ironically, it took a few more counseling sessions to help Mark forgive himself for unfairly blaming his parents for so many years.

The moral of Mark's story is forcing oneself to forgive or trying hard to "forgive and forget" isn't genuine forgiveness.

True forgiveness is more like an "undoing," a willingness to challenge and debunk false anger-inducing "realities" that get unknowingly triggered within. Once the truth finally emerges, longstanding anger and resentment can quickly and totally dissipate.

Mark realized his parents hadn't "betrayed" or "abandoned" him.

Upon this realization, his heart swelled with compassion and empathy...

Why was Mark angry with his parents for four long decades? Because he was entrenched in his own bullshit narrative about what happened and unaware of how wrong he was.

Why did he immediately redirect his anger towards himself?

The same reason—more internal bullshit, believing he should have spoken with his parents and corrected his mistake sooner. This, too, is an understandable but flawed philosophy.

Wayne Dyer would have counseled Mark regarding his parents, "They did what they knew how to do, given the conditions of their lives."

He would have conveyed the exact same advice to Mark as well. We can only act based on what we know and comprehend at the time.

To believe we "should have done something else," as Dyer points out, is "an absurdity." It's an equally poor philosophy whether we judge our actions or those of others.

Consider all the anger that festers worldwide due to this one absurd philosophy. Now, multiply it by countless other ridiculous beliefs, and it becomes clear why our world is populated by so many angry souls.

Chapter 33

In Chapter 2 (Anger At My Parents And Sister), I bared my soul, recounting the tumultuous relationship with my mother during my teen years and twenties. It was a period marked by conflicts that eventually led me to sever all ties with both my mom and dad for **seven long years**.

Over time, I realized my errors and managed to mend the damage.

Back then, I didn't have access to the knowledge about anger I can share with you today. The causes of my anger were a total mystery to me, and the Ultimate Anger Elimination System, which later became a cornerstone of my life, was only a distant dream.

I chose a path of personal development and received guidance encouraging me to question my habitual thoughts and responses. Through trial and error, I gradually learned new truths, even without a formalized framework and system like you have gained by reading this book.

My discontent lay in my mom's inability to accept my growing independence. She persisted in treating me as a child, offering unsolicited advice and insisting I accept extra food from her at every family meal. The constant friction fueled my anger, and I kept trying to make her change. Each time my efforts proved fruitless, my anger intensified.

The straw that broke the camel's back came when she called and offered unwanted medical advice. My anger reached its zenith, and I decided to get off the emotional rollercoaster—and never step back on it.

During most of those seven years of self-imposed isolation from my parents, I had no intention of ever returning. My anger felt insurmountable, and I had no faith in my ability to control it in their presence.

A Slow Awakening

During the last six months of this exile, however, something changed within me. Intuitively, I started to comprehend the three internal filters driving my anger. Without a formal framework or system to bring them to my attention, I began questioning these filters and sought deeper truths.

One of the first notions I challenged was whether it was truly wrong for my mother to persist in treating me as she did during my childhood.

I realized she wasn't committing any crimes; she was trying to be a loving mother in her own way. She wasn't obstructing my growth, as I initially felt and believed. I had continued to grow and develop, even in her presence.

I also came to appreciate that her insistence on offering extra food was her way of saying, "I love you." There she was, attempting to communicate her affection, while my response was to push her away with a sense of irritation and disdain.

...she wasn't committing any crimes; she was trying to be a loving mother in her own way.

These new, more honest perspectives made my previous perceptions and behaviors less noble and justifiable.

I realized I had been on a multi-year mission to change my mother into someone she was not. It was a foolish strategy motivated by a misguided life philosophy.

With distance, maturity, and the wisdom life bestows, I recognized my approach was flawed from the outset. I realized my anger came from my own misconceptions, and my strategy to address it was fundamentally wrong.

As clarity emerged, I knew what I had to do. I saw that my anger and my need to escape it were both caused by bullshit.

Uncertain of my parents' response, I reached out to them, scheduled a meeting, and shared my new insights.

I apologized for not coming to my senses sooner and acknowledged the pain I caused them. It was an honest admission of guilt and an authentic acknowledgment of the suffering I had imposed on them.

Fortunately, their love for me had never stopped, which made reconciliation a smoother pathway.

From then on, I no longer harbored anger or disappointment towards my parents. My mother's attempts to offer food and advice didn't stop, but now they were met with grace and gratitude.

I saw that my anger and my need to escape it were both caused by bullshit.

What is the lesson here?

When someone consistently tells you they love you and they care about you, what is there to be angry about?

My mother lived to the ripe old age of 94, and her motherly behaviors remained unchanged.

What did change, however, was my perspective. I chose to adopt a new "filter" to view her actions. This filter allowed me to see her actions more accurately and remember what was true about them— and about her.

To download a copy of the tribute video I made for my mom to play at her funeral, go to **http://BestAngerCure.com**.

I n this chapter, I will introduce you to five anger elimination trailblazers.

These are coaches or consultants who heard me speak or otherwise learned about my anger elimination approach and saw the potential for their clients. They asked me to teach them the Anger Internal Causes Framework and Ultimate Anger Elimination System, and I agreed.

I will give a bit of background for each trailblazer and tell you what they do. Then, I share their answers to a set of questions I posed. Contact information for these courageous souls is in the Appendix.

Trailblazer #1: Karen Ross, Hypnotherapist

Karen Ross is a board-certified hypnotherapist and professional coach. She regularly helps people solve resistant problems like chronic pain, insomnia, weight issues, and quitting smoking.

Karen notes that hypnotherapy techniques have been used by some of the most celebrated and successful people in the world—Michael Jordan, Tiger Woods, Oprah, and Elon Musk, to name a few. It is also used by actors, performers, and even historical figures like Winston Churchill and Albert Einstein. Hypnosis is also used in world-famous medical settings like Mayo Clinic and Cleveland Clinic.

Karen also helps clients who are struggling with their emotions, including anger. This attracted her to learn more about my work, and she asked me to train her in my anger elimination framework and system.

Here are the questions I asked Karen and her answers:

Q: What percentage of your clients have anger issues that you address?

A. Once we delve into the root causes of whatever might be troubling a client, we almost always find an element of anger hiding someplace. It might be anger at a key person or situation in their life, past or present, or even anger at themselves for not being able to function as they would like.

Our goal is to transform that anger into a much more compassionate or forgiving emotion, which usually benefits the client significantly.

Q: How has Dr. Orman's Anger Internal Causes Framework helped you to better understand where your client's anger is coming from?

A. Dr. Orman's three-filter framework has given me new insights into human anger I can use to understand my clients' anger issues more precisely. Just having this framework available to me now has helped me to see anger from a new perspective that can help me better target my coaching and hypnotherapy interventions to improve and accelerate the healing process.

Q: Have you used Dr. Orman's framework and system to deal more effectively with your own anger issues?

A. Yes, indeed. We've explored some past and recent events in my own life, and I've been able to see and understand them better in a completely new way.

Q: How do you see Dr. Orman's framework and anger elimination system being helpful to you in your work?

A. It's another valuable tool to help me heal my clients struggling with issues related to people they think have wronged them.

It gives me a new angle to address this common problem and releases the harshness of the emotion of anger that keeps people stuck with chronic resentments.

Incidentally, Dr. Orman's approach is also very powerful for dealing with anger directed at oneself—another common problem I see in my work. This also makes it easier for me to accelerate this healing process as well.

Trailblazer #2: Leslee Montgomery, Wellness and Safety Consultant for Construction Workers

Meet Leslee Montgomery. Leslee is a Professional Counsellor, wellness and safety specialist, mental health advocate, speaker, and educator working in the male-dominated construction industry. She is the founder and CEO of Humanology Partners, a consulting and wellness company that creates blueprints for wellness and mental health for the trades.

Early in her career, Leslee became aware of trade professionals' unique wellness and mental health challenges. Her compassionate approach allows her to speak the truth and not shy away from tough topics.

Leslee's authenticity and years of construction work experience give her the opening and credibility to "hammer away" at the prevailing mental health stigma in the trades.

Mental health challenges can have a profound impact on construction workers and other physical laborers, affecting not only their work performance but their personal well-being as well. This can lead to diminished productivity, heightened aggression, and lots of pent-up and expressed anger.

Leslee asked if I would train her in my anger elimination methods. Here are her responses to the questions I asked her:

Q: Could you tell us about your journey to becoming a safety and wellness consultant, particularly in the construction industry? How did you get started, and why did you choose this industry?

A. *I was studying to become a paramedic, but as the mother of three young children, I eventually realized this career path would not work for my family. A classmate who worked in construction told me that the construction industry always needs people with first aid skills. With my paramedic training, I landed a job quickly. Initially, I was trying to survive in this new role, but later on, I fell in love once I realized everyone I worked with had a story that needed to be heard unconditionally.*

Q: What common anger-related issues do you encounter, and how do you address them?

A. *Most of the anger issues I encounter with construction workers stem from frustration with constant change and unexpected disruptions, lack of support from leadership, not having the appropriate equipment to do the work, and how poorly workers are sometimes spoken to.*

I am a listener at heart, so I always start there. Understanding that personal issues often impact work performance has been an enormous help when supporting others. Helping others clear their mind and see things objectively is where the magic happens.

Q: How do you build trust and rapport with construction workers who may hesitate to seek help for personal issues?

A. As a woman in a predominantly male workforce, I start by being authentic and approachable. Being responsible (in part) for worker safety can put me at a disadvantage. Sometimes, workers see me as a cop when it comes to safety.

Understanding that many people I work with are uncomfortable with vulnerability, I lead by example. Sharing what's going on for me and making space for those not ready to open up has been a game changer. When individuals see I am not there to force anything on them or demand that they open up to me if not ready, they are more likely to approach me when they are experiencing difficulties.

Many people assume the construction industry is full of male toxicity, but my experience couldn't be further from the truth. The construction industry is one of the most giving industries I have had the opportunity to be a part of.

However, like many other industries, we don't take our workers' mental and emotional health seriously. The reality is everyone struggles with mental and emotional health. We all fear how our actions or statements might be used against us. Given the right environment, most individuals will reach out for help.

Q: Could you share a memorable success story from working in the construction industry?

A. One of my favorite stories was hearing from a new crew I joined that I would be lucky to last 3 months. Two and a half years later, when the project wrapped up, I was sitting with one of the senior foremen who said I had helped him become a better man.

Q: As a professional wellness consultant, what was your experience being introduced to Dr. Orman's framework and system for eliminating anger?

A. Working with Dr. Orman's anger framework and anger elimination system has given me the pieces I was missing to approach anger more efficiently. Knowing there are always the same three "filters" or ways of looking at what's happening that are driving these moments of anger, regardless of who is feeling them or what triggered the angry reaction, gives me a new superpower for how to connect deeply with, and be of service to, each individual.

Already, I have included parts of Dr. Orman's teachings in morning meetings. Individuals get frustrated or angry during the day on a construction site for several reasons. Giving them guidance on navigating these emotions safely is very fulfilling.

I would love to see anger elimination and stress elimination discussed more frequently in our industry and individuals given the opportunity to practice using the tools recommended in a space that empowers them.

Trailblazer #3: Krys Pappius, Ex-Policewoman, Current Mountain Hiker and Women's Empowerment Coach

Krys Pappius is an Empowerment Coach, speaker, and best-selling author. In 2003, she was in her tenth year as an accomplished police officer in British Columbia.

As far as anyone knew, she was living the "good life."

Then, a serious car crash on the job woke her up to the reality that, while she had all the trappings of success, her life felt empty, and she no longer knew who she was or what she wanted.

At that moment, she promised herself things would change and that she would do whatever it took to create a life with meaning and purpose.

It took Krys several years of searching to discover the secret to creating the life she longed for, and that is interesting, purpose-driven, and fun. Along the way, she trained for and hiked Mt. Kilimanjaro.

As an Empowerment Coach, Krys' mission is to share what she learned on the mountain, in the police force, and in life with successful women professionals and entrepreneurs who are tired of feeling stuck and uncertain as they look to the future and who are ready to take action to create a life they love.

Here are the questions I asked Krys and her answers:

Q: How has your experience as a policewoman shaped your approach to life and coaching?

A. Law enforcement has taught me many things, some relevant to my work as an empowerment coach.

1. I know that EVERYONE's behavior makes sense based on what they know and what they've experienced in life. If a client is not getting the results she wants, I first have to shine a light on her subconscious and deeply ingrained beliefs about herself and the world around her.

2. I am not interested in telling people what to do. My passion is to help my clients tap into the wisdom and strength they already possess, and that will enable them to create a life that truly honors who they are and the impact they want to have on the world. I can teach them skills to help them move forward with clarity and confidence, but I cannot decide what is right for them.

Q: What drew you to mountain hiking, and how did it become an important part of your life?

A. In 1980, while visiting Kenya, I saw Mt Kilimanjaro—a beautiful snow-covered mountain towering over the flat African plains—from the window of an airplane while flying from Nairobi to Mombasa. I could not shake the magnificence of that sight. I learned that it was possible to hike to the summit and wondered what the world would look like from up there.

Climbing Kili was a dream I filed away for the next 25 years, dismissing the idea whenever it crossed my mind. Who was I to think I could accomplish something so extraordinary?

Then, in 2003, I had a near-death experience. The experience made me think of all the dreams I had said "no" to in my life and filed away on a dark shelf to collect dust. Hiking up Kili was right up there on the list. I committed to get to the summit, and in the fall of 2006, I did just that.

Being in nature and physically pushing myself made me feel more alive than ever. Looking at the world from the summit filled me with feelings of power, strength, and possibilities. Life was never the same again.

Presently, I live at the foot of the Rocky Mountains. I am surrounded by trails. Nothing makes me feel more alive, more in control of my life, than setting out on a trail, often on my own, to inhale the beauty, breathe the fresh air, and feel like anything is possible.

Q: How does mountain hiking empower you personally, and how do you convey this to the women you work with?

A. Being in nature, never knowing what to expect, having been caught in sudden weather changes, physically pushing myself—all these hiking components build my confidence and bring me inner peace.

Setting out on solo hikes was a big step out of my comfort zone. I was terrified the first time. I educated myself on how to do this as safely as possible, equipped myself with the proper gear, developed a safety plan, and now I am happy to set out solo.

I teach my clients that building self-mastery skills equips them to safely set out on their own journeys, whatever that may look like for them.

Q: Can you describe your coaching philosophy when working with women to help them rebuild their lives?

A. My philosophy is simple: I believe we all have a purpose in life: to share our unique gift with the world for the betterment of all. I believe we all have a depth of strength and wisdom beyond our wildest imagination. I believe we have a birthright to live life confidently, knowing we can deal with whatever life sends our way.

I believe we have a birthright to feel alive and engaged in everything we do. I also believe there are 3 steps to creating the life we truly desire, our best life:

- *self-mastery: knowing yourself at such a deep level that you get to choose, in every moment, your thoughts, behaviors, and actions (and this includes, among others, your core values and your purpose);*

- *vision: having a clear vision of what your best life looks like based on your values and your purpose;*

- *action: taking small baby steps that, in their totality, get you the life you really want.*

Q: What advice would you give to women who feel lost or lack purpose?

A. Too many of us look "out there" to see how we need to feel, think, and act to fit into society. The problem is that there is no consensus "out there," and it becomes crazy-making.

The key is to look "within," discover who you are at your core, and make decisions to honor that.

And, the most critical piece: it is NEVER too late to pivot from being stuck in a life you don't like to live your best life.

Q: As a coach, what was your experience being introduced to Dr. Orman's Anger Internal Causes Framework and system for eliminating anger?

A. After my near-death experience in 2003, I embarked on a journey of self-discovery. By the time I met Dr. Orman, I had been on that journey for many years.

I knew much about myself and what I was capable of. I had a good life, yet something in me was still in the way of a great life. I felt like there was a demon in me that needed to be excised.

What I learned from Dr. Orman is my demon was anger. Actually, it was rage. I experienced a lot of trauma and loss in my life, and I was angry—angry at the universe, angry at the world, angry at those who hurt me.

By implementing Dr. Orman's process, every time I felt anger, I was able to defuse the feeling. It led to a lot of forgiveness towards others and towards me. And with forgiveness comes effective problem-solving, new perspectives, and peace of mind.

Q: How do you plan to incorporate these new anger elimination insights and skills you now have into your work with clients?

A. The framework and system are both simple and yet so powerful. Dr. Orman has genuinely given me a gift that needs to be shared.

In today's world, where there is so much anger and conflict, teaching these skills to others is my small contribution to world peace.

Q: What would you like to see in the future regarding anger elimination and stress elimination training for women in general?

A. Far too many talented, intelligent, gifted women are under pressure to overperform, leading to anger, stress, and burnout. In an ideal world, this training would be available to young girls preparing to face a life that is often challenging.

I would like to see this protocol made widely available to men and women of all ages. As I said earlier, it is a contribution to world peace at the grassroots level.

Trailblazer #4: Mardi Winder-Adams, Divorce Transition Coach and Mediator

Anger and divorce often go hand in hand. Anger during a marriage can lead one or both parties to seek divorce. Then, the divorce process can bring in additional layers of anger. Once the divorce is final, chronic resentments and smoldering anger can last for years.

Meet Mardi Winder-Adams, an experienced mediator and now a Divorce Transition Coach who lives near Texarkana, Texas. Mardi founded Positive Communication Systems, LLC and hosts The D Shift Podcast and the Real Divorce Talks series.

For over two decades, Mardi has been helping high-achieving women find their path through the complex maze of divorce. She is known for helping clients find clarity amidst the chaos. She has a unique gift for assisting her clients in managing the emotional and financial costs that often accompany such a challenging life transition.

Mardi's own journey saw multiple career changes. She transitioned from teacher to domestic violence client advocate, to mediator and co-parenting trainer, and to certified divorce coach. Her success is a testament to her commitment to helping women through this critical life transition.

Her personal experience managing the stress and feeling overwhelmed by her own divorce equipped her with a deep understanding of her clients' challenges. She has learned and embodied the essential skills, abilities, and emotional resources needed to overcome the trials and tribulations of divorce.

Mardi's mission is clear: to ensure high-achieving women don't bear the overwhelming emotional and day-to-day challenges of the divorce process alone.

She offers the knowledge, support, and compassionate expertise every high-achieving woman deserves during this challenging life chapter. Her warm and professional demeanor, coupled with her immense expertise, makes her not just a coach but a trusted professional during divorce and beyond.

When Mardi learned about my anger elimination framework and system, she asked if I would train her so she could share these insights with clients.

Here are the questions I posed to Mardi, along with her answers:

Q: Can you tell us about yourself and your journey to becoming a divorce coach? What inspired you to specialize in coaching women through their divorces?

A. *My life took a big turn when I went through a divorce. This led me to seek training in family and divorce mediation in Canada. I also studied conflict resolution and conflict communication skills.*

After getting married again and relocating to the United States, I worked as a domestic violence client advocate, serving some amazing women who had levels of strength and courage I could only imagine. Eventually, I expanded my skill set and became certified as a divorce transition coach. It was evident that helping women through divorce was where I could make the most significant impact.

Q: Could you describe the range of services you offer women who are divorcing?

A. I provide personalized support tailored to each client's specific needs and circumstances. This means helping some clients explore whether divorce is the right path. Once we've clarified their decision to move forward with divorce, I work with my clients to help them select the right divorce attorney and know what questions to ask and how to assess which attorney's style will best suit their individual needs.

I also assist clients in addressing essential financial aspects during this transition. This can involve budgeting, managing day-to-day finances, and understanding temporary financial arrangements during the divorce proceedings.

Emotional support is another vital component of my services. I work closely with clients to address this aspect of divorce, which includes overcoming feelings of guilt and anger and navigating the grief process. I also provide a supportive space for making tough decisions and handling negotiations effectively.

Post-divorce, I assist clients in adapting to their new lives as single individuals. This phase often involves addressing co-parenting issues that may arise. Additionally, I help clients find clarity in their identity, addressing any limiting beliefs and emotional challenges they face as they embark on this new chapter of their lives.

Q: What are your core beliefs regarding supporting women during this challenging time?

A. I firmly believe in the power of active listening and thoughtful questioning. It's crucial for clients to feel heard and supported during a challenging time such as divorce.

I encourage clients to reflect on how they want to experience the divorce process. Do they value a low-conflict approach? If so, there are effective strategies to achieve that. Are they interested in taking an active role in the decision-making process, or do they prefer a more passive role, allowing their attorney to handle most aspects?

There is no one-size-fits-all approach to divorce. Each individual's circumstances are unique, and it's not my place to dictate the "right" or "wrong" way to navigate this journey. My role is to empower women with the knowledge and tools they need to make informed decisions that align with their goals and values.

Q: How do you provide emotional support to your clients?

A. I believe in creating a safe space for clients to express their thoughts and feelings. I assist my clients in delving deeper into the root causes of their emotions. We explore what's truly triggering their frustration, anger, sadness, or any other feelings they may be experiencing.

Many people believe that external factors or other individuals control their emotions, but in reality, we create our emotional well-being. I work with clients to help them recognize this power.

Q: As a divorce coach, what was your experience being introduced to Dr. Orman's framework and system for dealing with anger?

A. I first came across Dr. Orman's framework through a mastermind. Listening to him discuss anger elimination was incredibly inspiring, especially considering my background in stress management, divorce, mediation, and conflict resolution.

While many practices are excellent for managing anger and stress, they don't necessarily eliminate it. When I learned Dr. Orman offered training in his anger elimination method, I knew I had to become a student.

The training experience was fantastic. Dr. Orman guided me through addressing anger issues I had personally experienced as he introduced me to his powerful strategy. The impact was so profound I began using it with my clients almost immediately once I had the experience of using the method.

The feedback from my clients has been overwhelmingly positive. They've shared their astonishment at how effectively the framework addresses and eliminates their anger. It's gratifying to see it work for them.

Incorporating these new skills into my professional work has been invaluable. Given the nature of the coaching I do, anger issues often surface relatively quickly. While I don't typically start a divorce coaching session with a focus on anger, I'm ready to apply the framework whenever clients express anger or frustration. When clients open up about their feelings, I offer the framework as a tool to eliminate anger. So far, I have yet to have a single client decline the opportunity to learn about it.

Q: What would you like to see in the future regarding anger elimination and stress elimination training in the field of divorce coaching?

A. In my divorce transition coaching training, we did cover the topics of anger and stress, but it primarily focused on stress management and self-care, which are undeniably crucial aspects of the process. I firmly believe in the importance of self-care, as maintaining proper sleep, nutrition, and exercise significantly enhances our ability to manage emotions during challenging times.

What was missing from my training was a comprehensive approach to stress and anger elimination. There's a significant gap in the resources available for coaches, therapists, medical doctors, or anyone working with individuals going through divorce. Including stress and anger elimination training in such programs would be immensely valuable.

Trailblazer #5: Kim Groshek, Former Corporate Consultant and Creator of "Pause Power"

Kim Groshek is an elite business strategist and mental health coach known as the "Pause Lady." She is the CEO of Pause Power, Inc. She helps high-achieving professionals become more successful and happy through simple pauses that help ignite more focused results.

Kim's professional journey includes 35 years of leadership, innovation, and corporate success. She has excelled at project management, organizational design, and leadership coaching across diverse sectors, including healthcare, banking, credit unions, higher Education, manufacturing, government, and start-ups.

This wide range showcases her skill in driving impactful organizational changes and establishing robust systems and processes.

With two master's degrees—one in Management in Information Systems and another in Computer Science and Cognitive Science—Kim's educational background is extensive and well-rounded. Her Bachelor's degree in Education adds further depth to her academic achievements. She continues her Education at Cardinal Stritch University and Chicago School of Professional Psychology.

Beyond her professional endeavors, Kim has embraced yoga as a transformative practice. As a certified yoga teacher focusing on Ayurveda, Modification, Recovery, and Restorative Rehabilitation, she shares her expertise through online sessions, demonstrating her commitment to holistic well-being.

Kim has recently created Pause Power, Inc., a platform advocating the importance of pausing, connecting with one's inner self, and embracing one's true potential.

As the CEO of Pause Power International and Founder of the Spring Soiree Scholarship Foundation, Kim continues to be a trailblazer in empowering professionals and advancing women's causes globally.

Here are the questions I asked Kim and her answers:

Q: What attracted you to Dr. Orman's anger elimination methods and excited you about bringing anger elimination into your own work?

A. Dr. Orman's anger elimination system immediately captured my attention due to the potential to address the alarming rise in violence, rage incidents, and suicide rates. These are some of the most important issues of the mental health pandemic. Also, working with elite clients, specifically C-Suite Executives, exposed me to the unique challenges they face, with stress, anxiety, and anger impacting their daily lives and work.

For C-Suite Executives, the relentless pressure often leads to burnout. A 2022 Deloitte study highlighted that 70% are contemplating leaving their roles for positions that better support their well-being.

The concept of the Pause, combined with Dr. Orman's anger elimination tools, offers a holistic approach to reclaiming time and fostering well-being for professionals and others who could benefit.

By applying the Pause and eliminating anger, individuals could create space for more productive thoughts and actions. This process helps reduce anger, reclaim time, reduce stress and ultimately creates room for self-love. Integrating anger elimination techniques enhances professional performance and restores balance and well-being.

Q: With your 35 years of experience in the corporate world, how well would you say anger is handled in most corporations today?

A. The landscape of anger and stress reduction efforts in the business environment has evolved, but challenges persist.

On one hand, many corporations have made strides in recognizing the importance of addressing emotional well-being in the workplace. Some companies have implemented employee assistance programs, counseling services, and mindfulness initiatives to provide resources for managing stress and emotions.

Despite these positive developments, the corporate world still grapples with effectively handling anger. Hierarchical structures, intense competition, and the fast-paced nature of business often create high-stress environments. In such settings, emotions like anger can be suppressed or mishandled, leading to negative consequences for individuals and the organization.

Moreover, corporate leaders, including C-Suite executives, face challenges in dealing with their anger or the anger of team members. The high stakes and constant pressure in executive roles contribute to heightened emotions, making it crucial for leadership to model effective anger strategies.

As understanding of the importance of mental health continues to grow, there is an opportunity for corporations to invest more comprehensively in strategies that promote a positive and emotionally intelligent workplace culture.

Q: How do you intend to incorporate anger elimination principles into your Pause Power initiative?

A. My goal with the Pause Power initiative is to create a comprehensive mental health solution that seamlessly aligns with the needs of companies, schools, government entities, and organizations. I believe anger elimination is an integral part of this overall mental health improvement plan.

Q: With Dr. Orman's guidance, how difficult was it for you to add anger elimination strategies into your own life?

A. Incorporating anger elimination strategies into my life was remarkably easy. The simplicity and effectiveness of Dr. Orman's three-part framework made the process accessible and straightforward.

The simplicity of the method also meant that the individuals I work with could grasp and implement these strategies without feeling overwhelmed. The applicability of the principles to day-to-day anger situations allowed for a quick transition from theory to practice, reinforcing the efficacy of the anger elimination strategies.

The emphasis on practice was also a critical factor for me.

The ability to apply the concepts regularly in real-life situations facilitated habit formation, making anger elimination an inherent part of my daily routine. I have easily implemented these strategies into both my personal and professional life.

Q: Finally, what is your vision for the future of Pause Power?

A. My vision for the future of Pause Power is a widespread, transformative movement that liberates individuals, empowers families, and fosters a global community united by the shared values of intentional living, self-love, and genuine human connections. It is a movement that encourages everyone to regularly pause, reflect, and embrace the richness of the present moment.

Pause Power catalyzes a paradigm shift, empowering people to reclaim present moments, rediscover their true purpose, and cultivate a deeper connection to themselves and others.

Ultimately, my vision for Pause Power extends globally, transcending cultural and geographical boundaries. The movement becomes a force for positive change on a larger scale, influencing societal norms and encouraging a more mindful and compassionate world.

My thanks go out to all of these trailblazing leaders. I sincerely appreciate their willingness to let me share their stories with you. Please see the Appendix for contact information if you would like to contact any of them individually.

Part V

Proverbs 14:29

"Whoever is patient has great understanding, but one who is quick-tempered displays folly."

Proverbs 29:11

"Fools give full vent to their rage, but the wise bring calm in the end."

Ecclesiastes 7:9

"Do not be quickly provoked in your spirit, for anger resides in the lap of fools."

Chapter 35

By now, you've unraveled the web of myths and misconceptions surrounding anger. You've discovered anger isn't created by external causes but arises from within, from three specific cognitive and perceptual filters.

You've shattered the false dichotomy of expressing or suppressing anger, finding a third path—the swift dissolution of anger through my Anger Internal Causes Framework and my Ultimate Anger Elimination System.

You've witnessed the pillar of "once an angry person, always an angry person" crumble as my deep personal transformation four decades ago proves its falsehood. My work is also a testament to the many people I've guided toward shedding the weight of their anger over the years.

Moreover, you've realized the conventional approach of "managing" anger addresses symptoms and expressions, doing little to prevent the initial eruptions of anger.

Yet, amidst the myriad myths and misconceptions about anger, one particularly insidious belief looms—the notion that anger is not only reasonable but necessary, a vital aspect of the human experience.

It insists that you MUST have a certain amount of anger to be a good and normally functioning human being.

The Truth: A Life Beyond Anger

Contrary to these teachings and popular beliefs, you can lead a fulfilling and productive life with little or no anger included.

While anger may serve a purpose at certain junctures, propelling us to rectify injustices and assert our boundaries, it need not be a lifelong companion.

Even in the most positive contexts, once anger has sparked change or guided you toward a better path, there's no requirement to remain tethered to this destructive emotion.

The conventional approach of "managing" anger addresses symptoms

and expressions, doing little to prevent the initial eruptions of anger.

Embracing the equation ANGER = BULLSHIT reveals even the most beneficial anger, which once motivated you, also probably contained some falsehoods. It's best to acknowledge this truth and release the lies.

At times, anger may appear to still guard you or fuel your motivation, but beneath the surface, it gnaws at your well-being.

My journey to the Grand Canyon helped me understand negative emotions can be relentless destructive forces.

When I first stood at the canyon's rim and looked in, its breathtaking beauty and immense grandeur stirred an intense emotional response within me. It was an overwhelming reaction that puzzled me, considering it was just a geological wonder—a hole in the ground.

Yet, what I failed to see initially was I wasn't merely gazing into a canyon; I was standing in front of the passage of millions of years of TIME and CHANGE. That's something you can powerfully FEEL.

The river that now flowed at the canyon's base once occupied the very level where I stood. Over eons, it eroded away the earth, shaping the awe-inspiring landscape I beheld.

In the same way, anger and stress erode our lives slowly and imperceptibly.

Day by day, little by little, anger eats away at our health, relationships, happiness, and the very essence of our existence. It operates in the background, subtly eroding and diminishing our well-being.

…anger and stress erode our lives slowly and imperceptibly.

So, despite any utility anger may have had in the past, there's no need to embrace it as a friend. Anger is an insidious force, slowly consuming us.

By embracing the anger elimination framework and system outlined in this book, you can release your anger and minor irritations, paving the way for a happier, healthier life.

In the next chapter, we'll explore how the principles you've learned here can contribute to maintaining a thriving and harmonious marriage and family life.

Chapter 36

Ah, relationships—a rollercoaster of emotions filled with joys and challenges.

We spend much of our lives searching for love, striving for intimacy, and assessing potential life partners. Yet, despite our best efforts, many of these relationships crumble, leaving us wondering why.

Why is it that we, as humans, frequently destroy the very bonds we work so hard to create?

The answer often lies in the insidious presence of anger.

We become angry with our partners, children, friends, and even our loyal pets. The consequences can be dire, especially when children are involved. So, why does this pattern repeat itself?

The answers are multifaceted, and in this chapter, we will explore the good and bad reasons for this common occurrence.

First, there are the bad reasons—the belief that anger and heated arguments are part of a "healthy" relationship and that love inevitably leads to anger. These notions are pure, unadulterated bullshit. They are misconceptions about nurturing a thriving, long-term partnership, but that's a topic for another book.

This chapter focuses on understanding why anger permeates our relationships and how we can rectify this.

Before we dive into this crucial topic, let's take a light-hearted detour. I've compiled a few funny quotes about marriage and relationships to remind us that while relationships can be enriching, they are not easy:

1. "Marriage is when a man and woman become one. The trouble starts when they try to decide which one." – Anonymous

2. "I love being married. It's so great to find that one special person you want to annoy for the rest of your life." - Rita Rudner

3. "Marriage is like a deck of cards. In the beginning, all you need is two hearts and a diamond. By the end, you're looking for a club and a spade." – Anonymous

4. "A successful marriage requires falling in love many times, always with the same person." - Mignon McLaughlin

5. "I asked my wife, 'Where do you want to go for our anniversary?' She said, 'Somewhere I haven't been in a long time!' So, I suggested the kitchen." – Anonymous

6. "Marriage is the bond between a person who never remembers anniversaries and another who never forgets them." - Ogden Nash

7. "Behind every great man, there is a woman rolling her eyes." - Jim Carrey

8. "Love is blind, but marriage restores its sight." - Georg C. Lichtenberg

9. "The secret of a happy marriage remains a secret." - Henny Youngman

10. "Marriage is the only war in which you sleep with the enemy." - François de La Rochefoucauld

Now, back to business.

The root cause of excessive anger in our relationships is not difficult to find. Just revisit our three-filter framework for identifying the internal causes of anger:

- Filter 1: Someone did something bad or wrong they shouldn't have done.

- Filter 2: Someone was hurt, harmed, disappointed, or negatively impacted.

- Filter 3: The offending person was solely responsible or to blame.

This framework encapsulates why we experience so much anger in our relationships.

The root cause of excessive anger in our relationships is not difficult to find. Just revisit our three-filter framework for identifying the internal causes of anger.

When we transition from living independently to committing to another person, we open the door to countless opportunities for conflicts.

You want one thing; your partner wants another. You suggest a restaurant; your partner vetoes it. You seek meaningful conversations; your partner prioritizes differently. You plan a family gathering; your partner prefers to avoid your parents.

These constant differences lead to negative judgments, blame, hurt feelings, and, inevitably, anger.

The critical aspect to acknowledge is most of these judgments, blame, and hurt feelings are based on bullshit.

You may have unrealistic expectations, judge your partner's actions unfairly, or refuse to reconsider your established beliefs.

If you observe your behavior within a relationship, you'll often find yourself in a sea of judgment, blame, and disappointments. Irritation and anger naturally follow from these feelings.

The secret to eradicating anger from your relationships is consistently applying the framework and system we've discussed. Once you identify your invisible anger causes, you can tackle them head-on with the Ultimate Anger Elimination System— CONFIRM—SUSPECT—SEARCH—CORRECT.

Use the Ultimate Anger Elimination System to investigate how your automatic thoughts, perceptions, and behaviors fuel your anger.

Instead of defending and justifying your beliefs, be open to the possibility of being wrong—what an unusual idea?

In a healthy relationship, the first person to get angry and then admit their mistake wins—and so does the relationship.

Anger And Your Children

Let's shift our focus to the impact of anger on your children.

If you harbor anger issues as a parent, you may unintentionally harm your children. While kids are resilient, they can also be permanently scarred by their parents' emotional expressions.

To ensure your children grow into healthy, well-adjusted adults, you must learn and model emotional self-regulation for them.

If you harbor anger issues as a parent, you may unintentionally harm your children.

Master the principles of anger elimination revealed in this book and strive to minimize judgment and blame directed at your kids.

As they grow older and more understanding, leave a copy of this book where they can find it. It may help them navigate their own emotions and relationships more successfully.

Remember, a fulfilling, anger-free relationship is not a pipe dream—it's a possibility within reach.

By acknowledging and addressing the **internal causes** of your angry feelings and reactions, you can transform your relationships and protect the well-being of your loved ones.

Chapter 37

The Unrecognized Value of Suspecting You May Be Wrong

In this chapter, I share a life mastery principle that may challenge your preconceptions but can potentially transform your life profoundly.

This is the second longest chapter in the book (Chapter 34 Anger Elimination Trailblazers is longer). Its length mirrors the significance and depth of the principle at hand. This principle, which lies at the core of the Ultimate Anger Elimination System, can revolutionize your relationship with anger.

In 2011, I penned an article titled:

"The Single Most Important Thing You Can Do To Reduce Anger And Stress In Your Life" © 2011 By Morton C. Orman, M.D.

The article began like this:

Dear Reader,

Congratulations. In this article, I will reveal the most crucial action you can take to diminish anger and stress in your life—now and for the rest of your days.

Before stumbling upon this insight, I mainly lived in a state of anger, frustration, and discontent. I felt ill at ease in social settings, and my personal relationships also suffered.

While my career as a physician thrived, I couldn't fully relish my success because of so much emotional turmoil.

Then, I grasped the insight I'm about to share with you—and everything shifted. This one revelation transformed my existence.

The change in me wasn't immediate, but I knew I was charting a new course. With time, I began shedding my anger, anxiety, and frustration. My relationships blossomed, and I experienced a newfound happiness and tranquility.

This single insight led me to conquer my anger and stress issues, which had plagued me for years and equipped me to guide others effectively as an anger and stress coach.

I nicknamed this core principle "the Mother of all stress tips" because it is the most potent personal growth revelation I've ever encountered.

Suppose you choose to internalize this fundamental principle and explore its manifold implications. In that case, your capacity to eliminate anger and other sources of stress in your life will skyrocket.

This new way of thinking can be applied regardless of your age or vocation. It will help navigate relationship conflicts, financial difficulties, work or educational challenges, and significant life challenges.

Some people understand this principle and harness its power to enrich their lives. However, despite its extraordinary potency, most individuals hesitate to embrace it.

This resistance comes from two places. First, you might balk at this insight when you first hear it. Second, deep psychological factors—

within us and our society—make it hard to accept this powerful life changing idea.

This one revelation transformed my existence.

What is the extraordinary insight I've been building up to? What timeless wisdom triggered such a monumental positive change in my life?

Here it is, encapsulated in eight simple words:

*"The most important thing you can do to reduce anger and stress is to...**learn to appreciate the value of being wrong.**"*

Eight words.

I assure you, there is nothing more formidable for grappling with anger and stress. No other piece of advice, be it single or collective, can rival the power carried by these eight words.

There is nothing more potent for tackling anger and the many stressful tribulations in life than acknowledging, openly and honestly, that you might be, and probably are, wrong about many things you fiercely believe.

Out of all the insights I've amassed to alleviate anger and stress, this fundamental insight left the deepest imprint.

It also proved to be the most challenging.

Obtaining admission to college felt substantially easier. Succeeding in college and subsequently in medical school seemed like a breeze in comparison. Even mastering the art of medicine and shouldering the responsibility of caring for others felt less demanding.

That's because none of these endeavors required me to appreciate the value of being wrong. In fact, they often pulled me in the opposite direction, reinforcing the universal human desire to be right at all costs while avoiding any specter of being wrong.

Embracing Being Wrong

The most important way to reduce anger and stress is to appreciate the value of being wrong. In that case, you can understand why this is so hard for people to do.

There is nothing more potent for tackling anger and the many stressful tribulations in life than acknowledging, openly and honestly, that you might be, and probably are, wrong about many things you fiercely believe.

Very few people see any positive value in being wrong. Instead, we hate being wrong and avoid it like the plague.

So, when I speak about appreciating the value of being wrong, I'm talking about something highly unusual in our society.

This major shift in your thinking might look and feel like this:

- Welcoming, not avoiding, being wrong.

- Viewing being wrong as your friend, not your enemy.

- Viewing being wrong as a virtue, not a sin.

- Being proud of yourself for discovering how wrong you've been.

- Feeling joyous about finding many more ways you may be wrong.

How Can There Be Any Positive Value In Being Wrong?

Accepting you may be wrong can benefit you by reducing your anger and stress and enhancing, rather than detracting from, the quality of your life.

But since you've built your life around being right—why would you give that up and begin to embrace being wrong?

How could you ever feel proud or joyous about discovering you are wrong?

And what does all this have to do with anger and stress, anyway?

---

since you've built your life around being right—why would you give that up and begin to embrace being wrong?

Before addressing these questions, I want to ensure you're not misunderstanding what I've said.

It isn't fine to be wrong in your job, or that you should build a bridge incorrectly, or feel joyous about making critical mistakes, or otherwise congratulate yourself for major failures, omissions, or other serious wrongdoings.

I'm talking about something different—I'm talking about what it really means to be human—and the inescapable role being wrong plays in each of our lives.

To Err...Is To Be Human

As human beings, we may be socially conditioned to want to be right. Yet, we are biologically structured to be wrong much of the time.

For instance:

• There are many aspects of physical reality (like oxygen in the air) that our bodies cannot see, touch, hear, smell, taste, or feel.

• Einstein showed that the physical universe is at least four-dimensional, yet our bodies can only appreciate three.

• Our eyes can see only a fraction of the total spectrum of light emitted by the sun.

• Our ears are incapable of hearing many sounds other animals readily recognize.

Our conceptual and psychological abilities are also limited in many ways:

• Our minds can focus only on a few critical aspects of our environment at one time.

• Our perception of events is limited to a small percentage of the total number of independent elements available to be perceived.

• While we've been taught to think about causes in linear terms (A causes B, which then causes C), life actually takes place in much more complex, multi-causal ways.

- While we've also been taught to think in either/or ways (e.g., good/bad, right/wrong, win/lose, etc.), these thought patterns are often inconsistent with the truth about reality (more on this in the next chapter).

Thus, when you consider what it really means to be human and how our brains and bodies are biologically designed to misperceive reality, you can see even the best and brightest among us are going to be wrong much of the time.

The History of Mistaken Ideas

Consider the numerous historical ideas that were once widely accepted but later proven patently false. Here are just a few:

- The sun and other planets revolve around the Earth.

- The Earth is flat…and venturing over its edge spells certain doom.

- Running a mile in less than four minutes is humanly impossible.

- Landing a human on the moon and bringing them back alive is unthinkable.

- The remedy for anemia involves leeches.

While it may be tempting to believe we've evolved beyond such erroneous notions, it's not so. We are as susceptible to error in our modern scientific era as people were in the past.

Even within our lifetimes, many accepted ideas have been debunked, such as the once-unthinkable sub-four-minute mile or landing a human on the moon.

In fact, much of the scientific "knowledge" I acquired in medical school almost fifty years ago has been disproven. Medicine constantly advances, rendering previous theories obsolete.

---

when you consider…how our brains and bodies are biologically designed to misperceive reality…even the best and brightest among us are going to be wrong much of the time.

The Link to Human Stress

What does all this have to do with anger and stress?

In my book, "The 14 Day Stress Cure," I highlight two fundamental factors underlying human anger and stress: **blindness** and **certainty**.

Blindness equates to our inclination to be wrong—and not know it. When we're mistaken about something, we're often oblivious to certain truths or realities that are not immediately apparent.

For instance, life isn't stressful; our filtered perceptions and reactions induce stress.

However, we are essentially blind to this truth, just as we are to various other hidden internal causes contributing to our anger and recurring stressors.

Blindness alone doesn't tell the whole story. There's another crucial factor at play—certainty.

Certainty represents our unwavering commitment to being right as often as possible and our reluctance to acknowledge the potential for being wrong. This commitment to certainty makes it challenging to recognize and correct our flawed biological, conceptual, and perceptual mistakes.

Blindness and certainty form a one-two punch that keeps us trapped in incorrect ideas and prevents us from glimpsing the truths that lie beyond them. We remain oblivious to this internal struggle, generating anger and stress as a consequence.

NOTE: With regard to anger, blindness and certainty correspond to steps [2a] + [2b] (blindness about internal causes) + [3] (blindness to the stamp of truth and the feeling of certainty it creates) in our four-step anger causation model.

Blindness also results from another critical feature of our internal filtering process, which I will explain in more detail in the next chapter.

Our Modern Age of Arrogance

Of the two primary causes—blindness and certainty— certainty poses the more significant obstacle for us to overcome.

It is our certainty—our stubborn, pigheaded, obstinate, inflexible, prideful, closed-minded, emotion-laden arrogance—that hinders us from acknowledging our pervasive blindness and making necessary corrections to compensate for erroneous thoughts, perceptions, and automatic tendencies.

Blindness and certainty form a one-two punch that keeps us trapped in incorrect ideas and prevents us from glimpsing the truths that lie beyond them.

How To Overcome Blindness and Certainty

The most effective approach to combat both blindness and certainty is to *embrace the value of being wrong*.

Instead of fervently clinging to your cherished theories, opinions, or firmly held beliefs and automatically assuming they are correct, relinquish certainty and welcome the possibility some may be erroneous.

Sometimes, you'll find your favorite beliefs are incomplete or partially misleading. Other times, the truth may be diametrically opposed to your long-held convictions. Still other times, after scrutinizing your cherished ideas for deficiencies, you'll discover they are well-founded and offer sound guidance.

Don't shy away from challenging long-held beliefs because of emotional attachment. Assess whether they serve you well or repeatedly lead to trouble. If they frequently cause problems…recognizing, identifying, and rectifying wrong ideas can yield immense benefits and significantly reduce anger and stress.

Consider the following:

• Embrace the idea that, as human beings, we are frequently wrong.

• Don't fear questioning the validity of your cherished ideas.

• Actively seek opportunities to discover mistakes.

• Foster relationships with people who provide honest feedback.

• Attend seminars or workshops that promise to expose flaws in your thinking.

- Read books or listen to content authored by wise individuals unafraid to challenge widely held beliefs.

In essence, *become a student of your own and others' erroneous or misleading ideas.* The more you do this, the more you'll realize how costly it is to neglect this practice.

The good news is that as you identify incorrect ideas, newer and superior ones will replace them.

Profiting from these improved ideas will eventually make you eager to anticipate discovering other areas where you've been wrong. An intriguing phenomenon will occur—your life's problems—including anger—will dwindle in number and intensity, and some may vanish entirely.

The Path to Success

Even with this approach, it's doubtful you'll ever let go of your desire to be right. This fundamental drive is deeply ingrained in us.

I know this because I have still not abandoned my desire to be right, though I believe everything I've just shared with you.

What I've realized is the most effective way to ultimately be right is to acknowledge just how frequently I can be wrong.

Our bodies and minds are hardwired to harbor false ideas and distorted "realities" that often lack a foundation in the real world.

Uncovering your erroneous beliefs about life can guide you toward being right (and successful) more often. This is precisely why I emphasize the value of being wrong.

When you embrace the understanding you've been conditioned to be wrong:

- By your culture

- By your family

- By influential figures in your life

- By your own flawed conclusions

You can correct these misunderstandings and move closer to being right, or at least more right than you were before.

A personal example will illustrate this.

From Repeated Relationship Failures to Ultimate Marriage Success

You already know I struggled mightily in my romantic relationships with women until my mid-thirties. Each relationship followed a familiar pattern: initial attraction, a cooling-off phase, escalating conflict, and eventual dissolution. This cycle repeatedly left me (and the other person) with heartache and disappointment.

While my anger issues played a significant role in these failed relationships, there were other contributing factors.

After each failed relationship, I would analyze and attribute the failure to some dysfunctional qualities of the woman I had chosen. And I would vow to never date someone with similar characteristics again.

However, after countless iterations of the same painful outcome, I began to suspect I might be the common denominator in these failures.

Even if I managed to overcome my anger issues, which I did, I realized I might still lack other knowledge and skills required to build and sustain a successful long-term relationship.

This suspicion that I might be fundamentally wrong about relationships in general prompted deeper introspection. I discovered that from a young age I had unconsciously adopted a formula for romantic relationship success:

1. Boy meets girl.

2. Boy and girl decide to have a romantic relationship.

3. The boy should dominate and always get his way.

4. The girl should endure this without complaint.

5. Boy and girl will live happily ever after.

What struck me about this formula was it had been silently shaping my thinking and actions for many years. Yet, I never saw it consciously or understood its detrimental impact.

This formula was a hidden internal source of my relationship failures and stress. Though I repeatedly blamed other factors, I never identified this insidious internal underlying cause.

Further examination revealed this formula wasn't a blueprint for success at all; it was a recipe for failure (i.e., it was pure bullshit).

I had mistakenly assumed it would lead to successful relationships with women when all it really did was produce a consistent pattern of relationship breakdowns.

This suspicion that I might be fundamentally wrong about relationships in general prompted deeper introspection.

The silver lining was *once I acknowledged just how wrong I was about how to succeed in relationships, I could avoid the traps set by this internal formula.* I consciously chose to learn about creating successful relationships, so I sought mentors to enlighten me on what I didn't know.

This led me to discover what does work to have good and lasting romantic relationships.

It also caused me to behave differently and treat my female partners equally and respectfully. I abandoned many of my destructive patterns, focusing instead on fostering mutual satisfaction and relationship harmony.

I've been happily married to my wife, Christina, for 39 years. And every day, I'm eternally grateful for being willing to admit just how utterly wrong I had been in the past about being a successful partner.

Other Examples Where We Frequently Are Wrong

We are similarly prone to errors in countless other areas of life. Here are a few:

- **Investing in the stock market:** Emotions, hunches, and unrealistic expectations often lead us astray. We buy when we should sell, sell when we should hold, and hold when we should cut our losses and run.

- **Marketing a product:** Believing in an idea without rigorous testing can lead to costly mistakes.

- **Low self-esteem:** Many talented individuals talk themselves into believing they are worthless, creating unwarranted negativity.

- **Lack of Forgiveness:** Frequently stems from erroneous assumptions or conclusions.

- **Blaming ourselves or others:** Often stems from flawed or overly-simplistic cause-effect logic.

- **Believing popular wisdom about anger and stress:** As we've seen here, many of these beliefs are misguided.

Now that you are nearly finished with the book, I can share a secret with you:

THIS ENTIRE MANUSCRIPT, INCLUDING THE ANGER INTERNAL CAUSES FRAMEWORK AND THE ULTIMATE ANGER ELIMINATION SYSTEM/METHODOLOGY, IS A COMPREHENSIVE LESSON IN THE VALUE OF BEING WRONG!

Every chapter is designed to illustrate how easy it is for intelligent, educated human beings to often be wrong, and how this leads to unnecessary and often harmful anger in our lives.

It's also causing all the hate, division, and violence we see and experience.

We shouldn't blame ourselves for being human; there is no need for negative judgments. It's just how our brains and bodies operate.

For instance, when someone says something negative about us, we automatically interpret this as a personal attack. These triggered, automatic responses are just part of being human.

The problem is we need to realize how frequently our triggered internal realities are wrong (for example, there may be some truth in the criticism). Thus, our reflexive defensiveness keeps us blind and clueless to the cognitive and perceptual filters and action patterns that are active within us.

This type of training in understanding ourselves better should be provided in elementary schools and then repeated in junior high and high schools. Since it's rarely part of formal education, we must seek it ourselves.

Maybe homeschooling leaders will seize this opportunity and provide the needed foresight and courage to make this happen. Hopefully, this book might become part of the curriculum in the future.

You've taken the initiative to enhance your understanding by reading this book. You are now equipped with a robust framework for pinpointing the exact internal causes of your anger, whenever you get triggered to become angry about ANYTHING.

Ultimately, it boils down to this:

THE AMOUNT OF ANGER AND STRESS IN YOUR LIFE DEPENDS LARGELY ON HOW SKILLED YOU ARE AT TELLING THE TRUTH AND RECOGNIZING HOW YOUR BODY IS WIRED TO DENY OR DISTORT THE TRUTH.

This book teaches you to recognize the internal causes of your anger. It provides a framework to help you clearly see these causes at work and enables you to take action to correct misguided beliefs or perceptions that may have led you astray.

Telling the truth is the way out, but it's a task only you can accomplish.

I can guide you in identifying the internal causes that generate your anger. Still, challenging them and freeing yourself from their internal distortions falls on your shoulders.

It's not an easy journey, but at least you now understand the immense value in SUSPECTING you may be wrong and how this wrongness relates to anger and stress.

As we approach finishing our journey, please continue to explore the concepts you've been introduced to here. If you take this training to heart, and put it into practice, you'll reap great rewards.

Thank you for allowing me to share my ideas and experiences with you.

Writing this book for you, especially this chapter, has been a genuine pleasure, and I hope it provides significant benefit. Please share it with others in your life, if you want to help improve their lives.

For a free, 1-page, downloadable PDF handout of "20 Huge Things Humans Have Been Wrong About" go to:

http://BestAngerCure.com

Chapter 38

Either You Think This Way...Or You Don't

In the previous chapter, I emphasized the profound value of acknowledging the potential for error, in general, in our thoughts, feelings, beliefs and perceptions.

In this chapter, I invite you to *adopt the practice of always assuming you are **wrong** when you experience any feelings of **anger**.*

In other words, I want to provide you with one more powerful reason to adopt the principle that ANGER = BULLSHIT and to never forget this life changing relationship.

Always remembering this key relationship is what unlocks a life free from the shackles of anger. This is the essence of why I penned this book—to impart this vital wisdom to you and others.

Why Should Anyone Embrace This Philosophy?

You might be wondering what drives the assertion you should consistently assume you are wrong (suspect bullshit) when anger surges within you.

The rationale stems from two fundamental insights:

1. Understanding the intricacies of our brain's evolution and functioning.

2. Recognizing how anger originates from the three anger-inducing cognitive-perceptual filters detailed in Chapter 21.

The Duality of Our Thought Patterns

Our brains evolved millions of years ago, becoming masters of rapid Either/Or Thinking.

In primordial times, lurking dangers and imminent threats demanded our ancestors make split-second decisions:

- Threat or no threat?

- Danger or safety?

- Friend or foe?

- Part of my group or an outsider?

Over time, our brains expanded this binary framework to encompass a wide array of additional dualistic Thinking:

- Good or bad?

- Right or wrong?

- Cause or effect?

- Credit or blame?

- Win or lose?

- Trust or distrust?

- Love or hate?

- Gain or loss?

- Heaven or hell?

- Believer or non-believer?

- An innocent young woman or an evil witch?

- Child or adult?

- Individual or society?

- Capitalism or socialism?

- Leader or follower?

- Man or woman?

- Straight or gay/etc.?

- White or black/brown/etc.?

- Smart or dumb?

- Yin or Yang?

- Western or Eastern?

- Republican or Democrat?

- Conservative or Liberal?

- College-educated or non-college-educated?

- Public/Private schooling or homeschooling?

- Climate alarmist or climate denier?

The list goes on.

The crux of the matter is this: if you are human, you are an Either/Or thinker. It's ingrained in your biology as an integral aspect of your brain's structure and function.

You cannot escape it, even with concerted efforts to transcend this ingrained mindset.

Either/Or Thinking permeates our society and constantly reinforces its influence.

Suppose you were born and raised in America or have lived there for an extended period. In that case, you've unquestionably adopted this pervasive thinking pattern.

And therein lies the root of your anger and many other life challenges.

...if you are human, you are an Either/Or thinker. It's ingrained in your biology as an integral aspect of your brain's structure and function.

The Perils of Either/Or Thinking

You may think, "Accepting we are naturally inclined toward Either/Or Thinking is one thing, but what's the harm? If evolution has favored this mindset, it must have its advantages."

Indeed, it does. However, it also carries substantial drawbacks.

One of the chief pitfalls of Either/Or Thinking is it blinds us (blindness) while simultaneously instilling unwavering certainty.

Remember from the previous chapter (Chapter 37) how Blindness and Certainty are primary sources of human suffering, anger, and stress.

Either/Or Thinking, also called polarized or dichotomous thinking, compels us to fixate on one side of a story, event, idea, or course of action while disregarding all or most other perspectives.

For example, if someone's actions appear right to you, how inclined are you to consider they might also be wrong?

When there's a competition, and one person emerges as the victor, do you readily view them also as possibly being a loser?

If an event unfolds in a way you perceive as good, are you typically open to the possibility it might also contain bad elements?

Our brains naturally avoid complexity, ambiguity, uncertainty, and confusion. They crave quick and efficient judgments, clinging to those perceptions as the definitive truth.

Yet, if you've lived any amount of time as a typical human being, you've undoubtedly encountered situations where Either/Or Thinking proved misleading.

Your experience with the media has taught you that if a news story only presents one side or one point of view, while excluding all others, it's a flawed narrative.

This is how Either/Or Thinking blinds us and leads us astray despite unwavering certainty in our convictions.

Connecting the Dots to Anger

Examining the three primary filters underlying our experience of anger, you can observe that each of them embodies a form of Either/Or Thinking (you may not have noticed this so clearly before):

1. Deeming someone's actions as bad or wrong implies they did nothing good or right.

2. Recognizing harm or negative impact suggests the absence of positive influence or benefit.

3. Holding someone 100% responsible or to blame negates the role of other factors or individuals.

These three internal anger-producing filters—the ones causing massive amounts of anger, hate and division around the world—are all Either/Or perceptions, rendering us oblivious to alternative viewpoints or middle-ground solutions.

Thus, it stands to reason that anger—ALWAYS caused by these three primary filters—ALWAYS comes from Either/Or Thinking.

This means anger ALWAYS comes from blindness, whether we are aware of this or not.

And routinely, no matter what we get angry about, our filtered views of reality lead to incorrect or deceptively narrow conclusions – in other words, it's ALWAYS "bullshit." Even when you think your anger is righteous.

...it's ALWAYS "bullshit."

If you understand how anger gets created inside human beings, you can appreciate that it always comes from bullshit. How could it be otherwise, given the Either/Or filtering mechanisms that generate it?

This is why assuming you are probably wrong when any form of anger surfaces **makes perfect sense.**

This also explains why individuals with genuine emotional intelligence, and not the trendy superficial version, *rarely assume they are right* when anger begins to stir.

Instead, they promptly disconnect from their automatic angry reactions, actively seeking to identify blind spots they might have missed.

When you train yourself to pause, disconnect momentarily from your angry reactions, and search for your own hidden blind spots, you'll invariably discover them. And when you get better and better at this skill, with practice over time, your anger will recede or dissipate entirely.

Recall once again the central mantra of this book:

ANGER = BULLSHIT

ANGER = BULLSHIT

ANGER = BULLSHIT.

By now, this no longer seems as eccentric or absurd as when I first announced it.

It's not just a saying. It's not just a theory. It's not just an opinion.

It's a biologic fact of how your brain and body actually work.

Commit to this mantra and you will discover how to have much less anger, hatred, irritation or resentments. Your life will also be enriched with greater joy, happiness, and inner peace. And, oh yes, your relationships and love life will thrive as well.

Part VI

From Jay Shetty, former monk, best-selling author, #1 health podcast host, life mastery and life purpose coach.

The truth is I didn't find myself until I discovered self-work, reading, and spirituality.

These 3 things changed my life more than anything else.

I began working on myself every single day and it gave me a sense of peace I had never known before.

I started reading like wild—self-help books, spiritual books, even the occasional fiction book—and it helped my brain calm down and open to the possibilities.

Most importantly, I started doing the self-work which EVERYONE must do in order to move forward and start living their best lives.

We all have pain. We all have self-doubt. But life doesn't have to be this hard.

When you make the conscious decision to work on yourself and live your life to your greatest potential…everything suddenly changes for you.

Chapter 39

Winners embody a unique essence—they consistently triumph. It's not just about believing you're a winner; it's about being in action, engaging in the game, and emerging victorious.

Think of Johnny Unitas, Tom Brady, Serena Williams, or other legendary athletes who etched their names in history through their unwavering commitment to winning. Consider the brilliance of Thomas Edison, Albert Einstein, Jonas Salk, Marie Curie, Jane Goodall, and the innovative spirit of Elon Musk.

Even the fiery John McEnroe found victory amidst his on-court tantrums, now transitioning his competitiveness to the pickleball court.

These luminaries, along with countless others across time and around the world, achieved greatness because they unlocked the secret to victory in their respective endeavors.

They became champions—just like Frank, Jim, Katie, Rick, Mark, and I became champions over our anger. Along with Brian Nowell, Ph.D., the author of "Anger Elimination," and others, we stand as testaments to conquering the challenging terrain of human anger.

I am eager for you to join our ranks, achieve victory over anger in your life, and shield yourself and your loved ones from its destructive consequences.

Within these pages, I've presented you with the tools and the roadmap to become a lifelong champion over anger.

You now have a simple, straightforward Anger Internal Causes Framework consisting of eight parts—with three being the primary focus—for pinpointing the internal cognitive/perceptual and behavioral filters that create and/or prolong your anger.

This framework is a priceless treasure that can become your steadfast ally for the rest of your life.

Additionally, I've provided you with a 4-step Ultimate Anger Elimination System, consisting of the powerful sequence CONFIRM—SUSPECT—SEARCH—CORRECT.

Once you get good at using this system, you'll see that its potency in quelling anger is astounding.

Within these pages, I've presented you with the tools and the roadmap to become a lifelong champion over anger.

By the way, this 4-step system is not limited just to anger. It works magic on other vexing emotions like guilt, frustration, fear, worry, sadness, jealousy, loneliness, etc.

The 4-step strategy remains constant—what changes is each emotion has its own specific framework of internal causes.

Just as anger gets created from filtered "internal realities" which often are not true, other negative emotions similarly originate from falsehoods lurking beneath the surface.

And as you've seen in this book for anger, each particular framework will guide you in how to root these invisible hidden causes out.

Regardless of what emotion you are seeking to reduce or eliminate, your mission, if you dare accept it, is to assume the role of an accomplished "bullshit hunter."

Unearth the counterfeit beliefs, unrealistic expectations, ill-advised counsel, misguided philosophies, fake news, brainwashing, and other error-ridden assumptions that underpin your anger or any other unwanted emotions.

In the end, what does it mean to be an anger champion? What does it feel like?

Being an anger champion means seizing the reins of this common emotion, no longer succumbing to anger's sway or permitting it to sabotage your existence.

You may not always prevent getting triggered, but you can swiftly extinguish the flames of anger once it begins to stir within you.

With this newfound mastery over anger, empathy for others occurs naturally. You will immediately grasp, with ease, the reasons behind others' irate outbursts—*because they come from the same three filters that cause your anger.*

You'll also understand how others could easily escape from the clutches of their triggered anger, if they could just discern the hidden filters inside them, and unravel them through CONFIRM—SUSPECT—SEARCH—CORRECT, which causes anger to dissipate, as truth replaces falsehoods.

It's also helpful to know that as you navigate this path, regularly practicing this approach, your mind and body will slowly change.

Months or years from now, situations that once incited your anger won't affect you as strongly as they do now.

This metamorphosis is the goal of the journey we've just begun together—you becoming a true anger champion. I've armed you with the required knowledge and tools; the choice to conquer anger now lies in your capable hands.

...as you navigate this path, regularly practicing this approach,

your mind and body will slowly change.

To grow your skill using the Ultimate Anger Elimination System (C.S.S.C.) and to spur you on to victory, here are additional tools for investigating and challenging your three primary anger-producing, Either/Or, cognitive and perceptual filters.

Filter 1: Someone or something did something "bad" or "wrong."

• Did they genuinely commit wrongdoing, or am I imposing my standards and preferences onto the situation?

• Could I view it as they did something "good" or "right" and see any truthfulness in that perspective?

• Is this transgression as significant as I think it is?

• Would I still find it important five or twenty years from now?

- Could there be positive aspects hidden within this perceived wrong?

- Can I envision a silver lining or beneficial outcome?

- Might both positive and negative elements coexist (the Yin and Yang)?

- Am I attributing negative motives without considering alternative possibilities?

- Am I offering the benefit of the doubt?

- Could I see myself acting similarly if I were in their shoes?

- Are my expectations realistic?

- Did the person perform to the best of their abilities, considering their background, knowledge, and maturity?

Filter 2: Somebody was hurt, harmed, or negatively impacted.

- Was tangible harm inflicted physically, financially, or in an irreparable manner?

- If only emotional "harm" is it significant, or could it be trivial?

- Could the apparent victim end up with any positive outcomes?

- Can they reframe the situation to minimize harm's impact?

- Am I amplifying harm beyond its actual magnitude?

- Could the affected individual reinterpret the situation, rendering it less consequential?

- Am I hypersensitive to specific types of harm and negative impacts?

- Have I been conditioned to perceive minor infractions as significant harm?

Filter 3: The offender is entirely or primarily at fault.

- Were they genuinely 100% responsible or at fault?

- Could I have contributed to the situation?

- Might others have played a role?

- Could genetics, brain development, mental health, substance use, or past trauma be factors?

- Can anyone be truly 100% at fault?

- Could external factors have influenced their behavior temporarily?

- Can we imagine valid motivations for their actions?

- Are we more focused on justifying our anger than exploring alternative perspectives?

These questions are starting points for challenging each of the three primary filters.

Remember, this inner work isn't easy or common.

Most people habitually believe in the infallibility of their automatic, triggered perceptions. Your challenge is to SUSPECT otherwise—to explore the possibility of error, and to hunt for hidden falsehoods.

As you travel the road of truth-seeking and expanded self-discovery, may your path be lined with clarity and enlightenment, and may your victories over anger be abundant.

Happy hunting.

Chapter 40

How We Can Create A Less Angry World

You now hold, in your hands, more than just a book; you hold a potent tool that can dismantle and conquer the specter of anger in the world, whenever it dares to rear its ugly head.

This tool has the power to transform you (and others) into a person who is far less prone to lashing out in fury, a person who excels at keeping your cool at work, speaking kindly to your children, cherishing and uplifting your partner, deepening your marriage, and avoiding the chaos anger creates.

Imagine the ripple effects. Imagine not just you but the next 1,000 readers of this book or the next 100,000 or even millions. Then, picture people across nations embracing and spreading these anger-reducing principles.

Can you visualize a world with far fewer angry souls?

I can, and I invite you to join me in creating it.

To advance this vision, we must share these core principles contained in this book throughout our educational institutions, from primary schools to home schools, and to universities.

We need to infuse this vital knowledge into the minds and hearts of healthcare professionals, wellness advocates, life coaches, business mentors, and educators of every stripe.

Anger elimination should be a recurring theme on global podcasts and talk shows. Training in anger elimination principles should be featured in wellness travel packages and permeate the orientation materials of college students, medical trainees, nursing candidates, and those entering many professions.

We must assemble an army of champions for anger elimination, advocates who will amplify the message far and wide.

Can you visualize a world with far fewer angry souls?

I can, and I invite you to join me in creating it.

You can contribute to this movement by sharing this book with those in your life you care deeply about.

If you're part of a corporation or large entity, give a copy to your company's top executives and HR leaders. Encourage them to explore how this wisdom can enhance the well-being of both leadership and employees.

If you participate in wellness classes or emotional intelligence trainings, spread the word about this book to instructors and fellow attendees. Let them know it holds the key to resolving any anger-related challenges they may be grappling with.

I invite you to become an ambassador for anger elimination.

It doesn't require Herculean efforts or take a lot of time. Seize opportunities as they arise, enlightening others about the prospect of liberating themselves from the clutches of anger.

There is a solution to longstanding anger issues, and now you have the knowledge.

Together, we can transform our world into a place where anger gets replaced by deeper understanding, compassion, and empathy.

Thank you for your unwavering attention and open-mindedness.

May your journey be marked by enhanced health, happiness, and success as you join me on this path to creating a less angry world.

A Heartfelt Invitation

Dear Reader,

Thank you from the depths of my heart for investing your time and trust in *Dr. Orman's Life Changing Anger Cure*. Your journey through these pages reflects a commitment to self-improvement, and I'm truly honored to be a part of it.

I've poured my soul into these chapters and shared every principle I've learned through forty years of dedicated study and practice.

You hold the complete distilled essence of my transformative ten-session Angry No More coaching program—nothing has been held back.

In Part IV, you saw real-life stories of individuals, much like yourself, who have embraced and mastered my Anger Internal Causes Framework and the Ultimate Anger Elimination System.

Their triumphs testify to the profound and lasting changes now available to you.

Some of you will use these insights immediately, forging a path to lasting inner peace and fulfillment. For others, the prospect of change may pose challenges that demand more personalized guidance and support.

If you need help applying these methods, you're not alone. I stand ready and willing to provide additional guidance, through my ten-session coaching program (one hour per session per week, over ten weeks), if you need or want more help creating a life free from the shackles of anger.

Consider this: what is the value of ten hours compared to the countless moments of strife and sorrow you can avoid by mastering the art of anger elimination?

It's an investment in yourself—an investment that promises immeasurable returns.

What sets my coaching program apart is the intimate exploration of your own unique experiences with anger—past and present.

Through this personalized journey, the tools and strategies given here truly come to life.

For those of you who can take full advantage of the blueprint for eliminating anger I've shared with you in this book, without additional support, I am truly excited for you.

Others, however, may want to explore how my coaching program can help you find a quicker path to inner tranquility. In that case, I invite you to take the next step.

Go to my contact information in the Appendix and send me an email message for a complimentary 30-minute Anger Elimination Consultation Call with me. We'll explore your questions and aspirations together and discover if this guided method aligns with your needs.

Your anger-free life awaits. Let's continue on this journey— together.

With heartfelt sincerity,

Dr. Mort Orman, M.D. – Anger Elimination Expert, dedicated to ending anger, hatred and division worldwide.

Appendix

Contact Details For The Five Trailblazers Profiled in Chapter 34:

Karin Ross (Hypnotherapist)

https://karenrossnow.com/

https://www.linkedin.com/in/karenrossnow/

http://MeetWithKarenRoss.com

Email: info@karenrossnow.com

Leslee Montgomery (Wellness/Safety Consultant | Construction Industry)

Company name: Humanology Partners

Website: www.humanologypartners.com

LinkedIn: linkedin.com/in/leslee-montgomery-976b78208

YouTube: Leslee is Awesome - YouTube

Email: leslee.m@humanologypartners.ca

Krys Pappius (Women's Empowerment Coach, Ex-Policewoman)

Website: https://www.kryspappius.com/

Email: krys@kryspappius.com

Facebook: https://www.facebook.com/crafter.krys/

LinkedIn: https://www.linkedin.com/in/kryspappius/

Mardi Winder-Adams (Divorce Transition Coach)

Company: Positive Communication Systems, LLC

Email: mardi@poscs.com

Podcast: The D Shift: Redefining Divorce and Beyond

Website: https://www.divorcecoach4women.com/

LinkedIn: https://www.linkedin.com/in/mardiwinderadams/

Kim Groshek (Business Strategist | Mental Health Coach | Pause Power)

Website: https://kimgroshek.com/

Social media = https://www.linkedin.com/in/kgroshek

Contact Details For The Author, Dr. Mort Orman, M.D.

Website: http://DocOrman.com

Linkedin: http://LinkedIn.com/in/docorman

Facebook: https://Facebook.com/docorman

Email: doc@docorman.com

Amazon Author Page (Doc Orman, M.D.):

https://www.amazon.com/stores/Doc-Orman-M.D./author/B00C0JNIW6

About The Author

Dr. Mort Orman, M.D. is an Internal Medicine physician with over 40 years of success as an anger and stress elimination expert. He has authored (23) and coauthored (11) books on how to eliminate anger and stress and has conducted hundreds of workshops for doctors, lawyers, nurses, business owners, corporate executives, students and even the F.B.I. He has also been the official sponsor of National Stress Awareness Month every April in the U.S. since 1992.

He is a graduate of Duke University (1969) and The University of Maryland Medical School (1973).

Dr. Orman's award-winning book, *The 14 Day Stress Cure* (1991), is still one of the most helpful and innovative books on the subject of stress ever written.

Dr. Orman, who was born and raised in Baltimore, Maryland, and his wife, Christina, a holistic veterinarian, now live in Florida, where their daughter Tracie also resides.

Made in the USA
Las Vegas, NV
08 December 2024

13642231R00155